MENTAL

Satanic Torments of the Mind

MARIE HEBERT

ISBN 979-8-89130-284-6 (paperback)
ISBN 979-8-89130-285-3 (digital)

Copyright © 2024 by Marie Hebert

All rights reserved. No part of this publication may be reproduced, distributed, or transmitted in any form or by any means, including photocopying, recording, or other electronic or mechanical methods without the prior written permission of the publisher. For permission requests, solicit the publisher via the address below.

Christian Faith Publishing
832 Park Avenue
Meadville, PA 16335
www.christianfaithpublishing.com

Printed in the United States of America

CONTENTS

Chapter 1: The Battle Over the Human Mind 1
Chapter 2: "What If…" 9
Chapter 3: Second-Guessing 29
Chapter 4: Splitting Hairs 47
Chapter 5: Obsessing 63
Chapter 6: Nay-Saying 79
Chapter 7: Commanding Demons 99

CHAPTER 1

The Battle Over the Human Mind

The Battle Over the Human Mind

MIND OVER MATTER

We have all heard them before: "You can do anything you put your mind to." "Set your mind to something, and you will achieve it." Another one is "Just make up your mind and *do* it!"

These axioms have been handed down to us from one generation to the next because of the powerful truth they contain. We have a tendency to downplay these tidbits of wisdom as mere clichés because we have heard them so often. We tend to minimize the efficacy of the message because the words are so common and so unsophisticated. We downplay, disregard, and deny the power of the message because of its unassuming little package. This is a grave mistake.

The truth is, our mind is a very powerful force. Our mind directs both our inward attitudes and our outward behaviors. Our mindset is what ultimately determines the ambitious success or utter failure of our weight-loss goal, our achievements in life, and our pursuit of holiness. This is because what we *think* is what we *do*. Is it any surprise, then, that Satan would want to control what we think?

Satan is working constantly to dilute and divert the power of our God-given mind. He accomplishes this by playing games with our thinking. Well, to *him*, it is a game. He works to sabotage our gift of reasoning. He aims to obstruct our rational, objective, and natural thought process. He plots to blur, twist, and warp our *perception* of facts to prevent us from making sound decisions. He knows that the way we humans *think* is the way we humans *act*. If Satan can pervert our thoughts, he can cause us to *act* perverted.

His goal is to confuse us. To overwhelm us. To discourage us. He wants us to feel inadequate. He wants us to perceive the world as being against us. He wants us to believe that God loves us "less" than He does other people. There is no thought, no idea, no memory, and no longing that Satan will not manipulate to cause us to act perverted.

The result of Satan's torments is that we humans seldom, if ever, live up to our full potential. Few of us ever accomplish the extravagant things that God has empowered us to accomplish here on earth. Hence, Christians have been dubbed the "Frozen Chosen" because we possess all this power and spiritual authority, but never use it.

Satan *wants* us to suffer mental torment. Mental torment is hell. Satan feels quite at home in torment. Mental stress from tormenting thoughts of uncertainty, panic, insecurity, and cynicism works to paralyze us in despair and inaction. If we could train ourselves to recognize when demons are speaking in our thoughts, we could then train ourselves to quickly remove them and their toxic influence.

CAN DEMONS ACTUALLY SPEAK TO PEOPLE?

The Bible is quite clear that demons do speak to people. They can speak to us both audibly and inaudibly. One such audible occurrence is recorded in Luke 4:34, between Jesus and a possessed man in the Jewish synagogue. Upon seeing Jesus, the demon inside of the man screamed out loud, "I know who You are: the holy One of God!" Jesus responded, "Be quiet! Come out of him." The Bible tells us that the people who witnessed this event were *astonished!*

The people were astonished—*not* because they heard a demon speak—but because Jesus had authority to command the demon to leave! The lack of horror on the part of the local townsfolk was because they were quite accustomed to hearing demons speak through people. There were local people *known* to be possessed. Up until this point, the local residents had to just "live with it." Up until this particular incident, they had literally never met anyone who could *do* anything about the demons! *That* is what astonished them!

Another audible demonic conversation is recorded in Mark 5:9, between Jesus and a possessed man living in the cemetery. In this particular conversation, Jesus asked the demon its name, and the demon answered out loud, "Legion is my name." The demon begged Jesus to cast them into a nearby herd of swine rather than commanding them to leave their assigned district. As the delivered man went about, proclaiming what Jesus had done for him, the Bible, again, says that the people were *amazed!*

Amazed at what? The people were *amazed*—but *not* because a demon spoke. The local people were *accustomed*, the Bible says, to hearing the demons screaming out of that same man, day and night. What amazed them was that Jesus was able to *free* this man—a man whom they had known his entire life to be unmanageable and incapable of being restrained because of the demons.

There are other biblical examples of demons speaking, of course, but it is not necessary to list them all. It is only important for us to take note that the bystanders, who were present during all of these audible exchanges—ordinary people like you and me—*heard* and *witnessed* demons speaking. The fact that not a single biblical account mentions that the witnesses to these events were ever shocked or horrified at hearing demons speak tells us that it was a common occurrence. It has always been a "given" that demons do speak to us.

THERE HAS BEEN A SHIFT

Demons, of course, do not always speak to us audibly. For the most part, demonic activity today has become covert and discreet. Satan's modus operandi has shifted from publicly *revealing* himself to *concealing* himself. He has gotten so subtle, in fact, that most people today, especially in America, deny that he even exists!

Satan and his angels do continue to speak and to influence people today, but now they primarily communicate with us inaudibly. Indirectly. Discreetly. This way, there are no witnesses. If we dare tell anyone about our dialogues with demons, we will almost certainly be dismissed as crazy. We will be mocked for "imagining" things.

But why the change? Why did Satan reveal himself so publicly and brazenly to humans *before* Jesus's ascension, but not after His ascension? I believe the answer is that there was a shift in power. The answer is a simple matter of who holds the most power.

When Jesus first came down to earth, humans had no spiritual authority, save for a few exceptional prophets here and there. People were clearly *aware* of evil—because the Bible records it—but they had to just "live with it." The Bible confirms that the townsfolk had become *accustomed* to hearing that man scream and howl, day and night, 24-7, from the tombs. But no one—*not even the priests*—ever commanded those demons to come out of that man. They did not have that kind of power. Demons did not have to obey them. Demons could do with men whatever they pleased because there was no one to stop them.

Pentecost changed that. *After* Jesus's ascension—at Pentecost—the Holy Spirit descended upon *mankind*. With Pentecost, the power of the Holy Spirit—the same power and authority that filled Jesus—now filled ordinary human beings too. Jesus foretold this when He told His disciples—men and women—to wait…they would *receive power* from on high *after* He returned to His Father.

As long as humans had no power to stop him, Satan had no reason to hide. He was a bully. The earth was his playground. He could freely roam about and terrorize people all he wanted without opposition. Pentecost, however, was the game changer. It literally changed the game when authority over the spirit realm was given to humans.

After Pentecost, the apostles went about healing the sick, raising the dead, and casting out demons on their *own* Holy Spirit power! They no longer had to keep returning to "check in" with Jesus. After Pentecost, they *themselves* were filled with the full Holy Spirit. Wherever and whenever they encountered Satan, they expelled him. *Every* time. *Every* where. *Every* day. Satan *had* to go into hiding! He could no longer afford to be so obvious. He was suddenly encountering humans who could fight back—and win!

Today, Satan is keeping a low profile. Gone underground. Biding his time… Most of us today simply "hear" him speak indirectly in the form of inaudible *thoughts*. Before Pentecost, Satan exercised his power for all the world to *fear* him. Today, he exercises his powers more discreetly because he wants all the world to *ignore* him. It is to his advantage to operate covertly today because he is able to make massive gains by remaining unseen in a world that no longer believes he is real.

The pendulum, of course, will swing back around one day; it always does. In the End Times, when the Antichrist rules the world, the Bible tells us that he will do so by performing great signs and public wonders for people to see. And people will be wooed because of what we have done to ourselves.

People in our world today have grown miserable *everywhere*. People are hurting *everywhere*. When the day comes that the Antichrist presents himself as the flamboyant healer and elixir for all our woes, the world will *rush* to follow him.

Oh, if only it were true. If only we Christians really were as "closed-minded" as the world accuses us of being. A mind like a steel trap would *never* let a demonic thought enter! The problem, of course, is that none of us has a mind like a steel trap. We are *not* closed-minded. Therefore, thoughts from dark spirits *do* sometimes enter into our thinking.

A thought, alone, however, is not *power* per se. Demons do not have the power to control our thinking. Even a person under demonic influence still maintains their free will which can resist Satan and *want* the demons to leave. Still, while demons cannot *control* our thinking, they can definitely *influence* our thinking. They manipulate the way we *act* by planting suspicious, negative, and fearful thoughts in our head.

Demonic suggestions are like squatters. Squatters are never *invited* in; they just *barge* in. They settle in and take over where they have no legal right to be. They are not necessarily there because of anything *we* have done, but because of *their* intrusive nature. They find a fertile spot in our brain—a memory, a hurt, a fear—and they will thrive and procreate there for as long as no one evicts them.

Our goal, therefore, in the following pages is to expose and evict them. This book discusses five primary torments—five demonic mind games—that I have personally experienced taking control of my thinking at various times. These mental torments—if allowed to squat in our heads—will cause us to move through life acting more like the walking dead than like the risen Lord. And that is precisely how Satan wants us to live: dead, lifeless, and impotent. Each of the next five chapters is dedicated to a specific one of these mental torments.

CHAPTER 2

The

Mental Torment

of

"What If…"

"What If…"

What is "What If…"?

"What If…" is a mental rabbit hole of dark, fearful thinking about our future. It is a demon-driven panic that keeps us fixated on *guessing, imagining,* and *envisioning* an endless litany of extreme and horrible things that could happen to us. "What if I can't…" "What if it doesn't…" "What if they don't…" This torment keeps our mental energy tied up in horror fantasies of the future to prevent us from preparing a rational, realistic plan of action. "What If…" overpowers our rational thinking to the point where we become convinced that a horrible outcome is certain, inevitable, and unavoidable.

FEAR OF THE WORST

We are most likely to experience "What If…" when we feel threatened by a sudden, dramatic shift in our life circumstances. Satan always employs "What If…" when we feel *forced* to deal with the possibility of abrupt, major life changes. For example, getting fired from our job. This is the one fear fantasy that has hounded me the most. "What If…" never torments us when the change in our circumstance is a change we *want* to happen. "What If…" only comes into play when we are facing an unwanted situation where we feel helpless to control the outcome.

When we perceive that threatening change is being forced upon us, we default to feeling helpless and victimized. The feeling of helplessness drives us to panic. Whatever the dreaded change in our circumstances may be, we can always tell when Satan is involved because of this one, telltale symptom: fear. Fear is Satan's signature calling card, and it will give his presence away every time.

Fear is the driving force and primary reason "What If…" is such a successful tool for Satan. In panic mode, our minds start bouncing all over the place, ricocheting nonstop between "What if this…" "What if that…" "What if this…" We quickly lose our bearings in reality and spiral into the realm of dark fantasy. Mental torment like "What If…" can drive a normally-rational person to become irrational and out of touch with reality because it is ignited and fueled by fear of the unknown. And fear—especially fear that is fantastical and demonic—is extremely combustible.

But…

"What If…," some people could argue, is merely a mental exercise in weighing all of one's options. Unemployment is a reality. Fear of unemployment is simply facing reality. After all, without a job, one cannot pay bills or buy food. Unemployment is a fact of life, not some imaginary satanic plot. In fact, it could be argued that it is *prudent* for people to think about, and to prepare for, the possibility of hard times ahead. Unemployment is a realistic possibility for everyone. Every time we come to an unexpected crossroad in life, the critics argue, does not automatically mean that something demonic is going on. They make a valid argument.

First of all, there is nothing imaginary about a looming threat of unemployment. Secondly, Christians actively engaged in spiritual warfare are often mocked by the world as imagining Satan behind every bush and under every rock. We are often accused of seeing him everywhere we turn, and blaming him for everything that goes wrong, in every inconvenient circumstance, even for those things that are merely a "fact of life."

While we do not, contrary to what the skeptics think, see Satan behind every bush and under every rock, we cannot ignore the very real "fact of life" that these *are* his usual hiding places. So, while we should not automatically rush to blame Satan as the cause of all our troubles, we should not automatically rush to rule him out either. Fortunately, there *are* concrete, objective ways that we can discern when Satan is controlling our thoughts with "What If…"

How to Recognize Satan

First, ricocheting between all of these gloom-and-doom fantasies is *not* the same thing as "weighing all of our options." We can differentiate satanic "What If..." from natural "weighing all of our options" by the imbalance. "What If..." is one-sided, while "weighing all of our options" is two-sided.

When we are truly weighing all of our options, we will have both good *and* bad options to weigh. We weigh *both*—the "Pro's" *and* the "Con's." *That* is "weighing *all* of our options"! When "What If..." is controlling our thoughts, there are *never* any "Pro's." *All* of our options are bad. "*What if* I cannot find another job? *What if* I lose my home? *What if* my friends abandon me?..." This is the first way that we can recognize a satanic attack—our options are exclusively one-sided. *All* of the options are negative.

A second way we can confirm that "What If..." is satanic is by its unnatural pace. The sheer pace at which these horrifying scenarios flash across our mind is unnatural. Even on a good day, most of us cannot think this frantically, this feverishly, or this compulsively. This simply is not how God designed our human mind to function. Our thoughts, when under the influence of "What if...", flash abnormally fast. It is neither human nor natural for our minds to churn like a strobe light. We only think this way—in *panic-and-manic* mode—when we are under spiritual attack.

The third sign that Satan is controlling our thoughts is the compulsive nature of our worrying. Not only are we imagining only gloom-and-doom, and imagining it at a frantic pace, but we *cannot stop*. We no longer control our own thoughts. We cannot find the brake, the off switch, or the breaker box to shut it down. We are unable to "shelf" these consuming thoughts long enough to get any sleep. The squatters have taken over, and they will not leave!

A fourth way we can recognize that "What If..." is satanic is by our being blocked from having any conscious thoughts of God. Under the influence of "What If...", the Knight in shining armor never arrives, the Good Guy in the white hat never enters the picture. "What If..." will never allow us to imagine ourselves being rescued. Only Satan would want to blot out God as an option in a crisis. "What If…" keeps us so overwhelmed and preoccupied with gloom-and-doom that we forget about God. *Worrying* unceasingly blocks us from *praying* unceasingly.

Finally, the fifth test of discernment that proves "What If…" is a satanic attack is its fruit. This is the ultimate test for just about everything in life. Jesus told us that we are to judge *all* activities, *all* experiences, *all* thoughts, and *all* relationships by their fruit. Personally, when I get caught up in "What If…", I feel panicked, doomed, and abandoned. I *never* feel that way when I am under the influence of God's presence.

OUR PARENTS ARE GETTING DIVORCED

My parents, like everyone else's parents, sometimes argued. For the most part, however, they kept their arguments private. They somehow managed to keep it together in front of us children. Well, except for this one time when all hell broke loose.

My two brothers and I had no idea what their argument was about, and I still do not know. At the time, we were too young to comprehend the concept of money management. Too innocent to grasp the pain of infidelity. Too naive to understand the frustrations of a mother *forced* to stay home all day and a father who was never *allowed* to stay home all day. We children had no earthly idea why our parents were screaming at each other in such an unprecedented way. Whatever it was, though, we knew it had to be something dreadfully bad.

All three of us children simultaneously ran into our laundry room to hide. How we all knew to run to the same place remains a mystery. We ran as if practicing a fire drill. At the sound of the fire alarm, everyone is supposed to know where to run, except that our family had never before practiced a fire drill.

Once in the laundry room, the three of us dropped to the floor, and huddled together in a circle. We were too afraid to make a sound. At that moment, we were afraid of our own parents. I heard my father yell something about how *he* had a job and *he* could survive, but *she* had nowhere to go and no way of supporting herself. Not only that, but no one would want her with *us* three children.

My older brother is only one year older than myself. So he could not have been more than eight or nine years old at the time. He was no more experienced in surviving life-threatening situations than I was. Still, he was the oldest, so it fell to him to keep the rest of us alive. I whimpered to him, "What's going to happen to us?"

He began brainstorming different options—different relatives with whom we might live. Never having experienced divorce before, it never occurred to us that we would continue living with one of our parents. As he whispered one scenario after another, our innocent minds were forced to wrestle with a litany of insurmountable, dead-end obstacles.

How would we physically get there? None of us could drive.

One aunt already had kids of her own to feed.

Our bachelor uncle did not know what to do with children.

Our aunt on the next street would probably return us.

Granny was too old.

What if no one wanted us? *What if* we were separated? *What if* we never saw each other again—*ever*—for the rest of our lives? *What if* our dog ended up in the pound? We frantically raced through multiple gloom-and-doom scenarios, one after the other, searching for one in which all of us could survive together—*with* our dog!

The one thing of which we all were certain was that our lives were "over." We would never have a Mamma or Daddy again. Our young imaginations were straining to see into a future whose forecast was dark and foreboding. That moment, locked together in a trembling embrace, was certain to be the last time we would ever be a family. Our own parents did not want us anymore. We *had* to find another place to live or we would die. Our dog was going to die too.

I do not remember their argument ending. I do not remember Daddy leaving. I do not even remember coming out of the laundry room. All these years later, all I remember of that day was the loud screaming and the overwhelming panic. I remember the terrifying scenarios of all the bad things that were *certain* to happen to us. No matter the scenario, they *all* ended badly for us—and for our dog.

This childhood experience of mine parallels our adult experience with "What If..." This satanic torment has the same distinguishable characteristics regardless of its victim's age. It force-feeds gloom-and-doom scenarios at a flash-flood pace. It is characteristically one-sided, manic, and uncontrollable. No matter whom its prey, the only thing its victim can imagine under its influence is the absolute worst, the most bizarre, the most far-fetched, and the most devastating thing that could ever possibly happen to them.

My parents did not get a divorce. When Daddy left, he only left to go to work. Our dog lived comfortably with us into his old age. And we children continued to play and squabble with each other up until we were old enough to leave home. *None* of the horrible things we envisioned that day happened. It was all in our imaginations—exaggerated and blown out of proportion.

THEREFORE, the first thing we must do to stop "What If…" is to try to collect ourselves. The *effort* to collect ourselves is spiritual warfare. We need to regain our emotional, physical, and spiritual composure as quickly as possible because we can lose our grip on reality very quickly. The five signs listed above for recognizing Satan's presence are an objective checklist against which we can gauge when our thinking is caught up in a game with dark spirits. We all like to *think* that we are rational, "in control" people. The truth, however, is that we are almost *never* capable of looking at ourselves objectively.

When the five conditions above are present, Satan is *already* in our head. He is not attacking us to *gain* control; he is *already* in control. Under the influence of "What If…," we entertain thoughts that are "crazy" in that they are extreme, hysterical, and far-fetched. The only options Satan shows us are the bizarre, fatalistic, and highly improbable ones. Our fears *feel* real, even though they are not realistic.

When our fears start sounding un-realistic, un-likely, and un-natural, we are often dismissed by others as being hysterical. And people tire of hysteria very quickly. No one wants to deal with the drama—not even our friends. People will quickly wash their hands of us, compounding our feelings of helplessness. We lose credibility with our peers. My life has certainly proven this to be true.

THEREFORE, the second thing we can do to stop "What If…" is to resist the temptation to run to other people for the solution. Other people are usually more helpless than we are. "Run to the throne, not to the phone" as Rick Warren says. This is not to say that we cannot *confide* in our friends; it simply means that our solution is seldom found in them.

"What If…" overwhelms us with feelings of abandonment and helplessness. We cannot envision our escape, only our demise. "What If…" *never* allows us to imagine a positive way out of our circumstance. Its modus operandi is to *block* our view of any positive ending. It blocks us from picturing God in our crisis. "What If…" works like a pair of dark sunglasses—its purpose is to block the Son from our eyes!

THEREFORE, the third thing we can do to end "What If…" is to *decide* to picture God in our circumstance with us. This step requires determination. We must *force* ourselves to seek God. We cannot simply *wait* for God to show up and chase away the boogeyman. We need to reach out to grab on to Him—like my brothers and I grabbed on to each other in that laundry room. It will have a steadying effect on us. We must never lose sight of the fact that God *saw* our crisis coming. He saw it *years* in advance. This means that, by the time the crisis materializes in our human time, God has already set its solution in motion.

"What If…" works quickly. This is why we feel so overwhelmed. "What If…" flashes multiple demoralizing scenarios—as many as possible, as fast as possible—across our mind. We have no time to work through one hopeless scenario before another one overwhelms us. Our cognitive functions become backlogged. It is too much, too fast, and with too little time to realistically think through each possible scenario. This is why we feel so overwhelmed.

THEREFORE, the fourth thing we can do to stop "What If…" from controlling our thinking is to take frequent breaks. We must get out of panic mode, even if for only a few moments. We need to get off the merry-go-round in order to clear our dizzy head and regain our objectivity. We need to do a manufacturer's reset and start fresh. We can go to a movie. Notice how green the grass is. Look for faces in the clouds, etc.

This is not an exercise in minimizing or denying the seriousness of our situation. This is necessary, routine maintenance. We are giving our mind its needed rest in order to break the grip of "What If…" It is part of taking care of ourselves, physically and mentally.

Forcing ourselves to clock out and take a break is how we clear and refresh our mental acuity.

I still do wrestle sometimes with "What If…" at the resurgence of threats of firings at work. Then I become angry with myself for not having more faith than that. I get disappointed with myself for not being "holier" than that. I beat myself for not reacting more spiritually "advanced" than that. Satan starts telling me that God, too, is disappointed in me. I scold myself for having learned "nothing" in all these years. Satan simply will never stop lying to us…

THEREFORE, the fifth thing we can do to stop "What If…" is to stop listening to it. God once told me, "When Satan steps up to the podium, just unplug the microphone!" Satan cannot influence our thinking if we cannot hear him. We can tell him to shut up. Literally—not figuratively. We should say out loud, "Satan, SHUT UP! In the Name of Jesus, I *forbid* you to communicate with me!" Because Christ's authority is now in us, Satan *must* obey us, just as if it were Jesus Himself commanding him to be silent.

The Purpose of "What If…"

The purpose of "What If…" is to unravel our faith in God. Satan aims to keep us *feeling* so abandoned, *feeling* so helpless, and *feeling* so hopeless that we no longer *feel* that God cares what happens to us. Satan aims to portray God as the absent Father who is never around when we need Him.

Fear throws up these big mental flash cards in front of our face. On each flash card is printed in large, bold capital letters, "WHAT IF…" It is hard for us to see God when Satan blocks our line of sight with his flash cards. Just as the earth's sun can be temporarily eclipsed by a passing cloud, so can our awareness of God become eclipsed when something dark and ominous blocks our view of Him. The goal of "What If…" is to cause us to despair to the point of feeling like we are "nothing" to God. Satan tells us that God has abandoned us so that we, in our hysteria, will abandon God in return.

The fact that we all sometimes wrestle with "What If…" does not mean that we lack faith. We *do* have faith; it is just imperfect. Let us not be too hard on ourselves. Faith and doubt are both measured on the same sliding scale. We have, at any given moment, components of *both* operating in us simultaneously. Did not the man in Mark's gospel cry, "Lord, I *do* believe. Help my unbelief"?

THEREFORE, the sixth thing we can do to end "What If…" is to ask God for *evidence* of His presence. We can ask for proof. This is not "testing" God. Asking to *feel* God's presence is a prayer. It is a prayer born out of our deepest need for relationship with Him. "Lord, show me the evidence of Your presence here with me."

How This Mind Game Works

At my current job, we are threatened every single day with being fired. This is how my employer manages: by intimidation. There have been many times when I have become panic-stricken, *convinced* that I was going to be the next one fired. It was during one of those panic-and-manic times that God spoke to me regarding how "What If…" works:

HALL OF MIRRORS

Fear works mostly by illusion. You do not even *know* concretely what it is that you are supposed to be afraid of! Fear distorts reality. Fear distorts reality so that you have nothing realistic and accurate to stay focused on.

Fear surrounds you on all sides as in a Hall of Mirrors. Each mirror shows you an exaggerated, distorted hallucination of things that could possibly go wrong. You keep spinning in circles, trying to get out, but everywhere you turn, you find only another mirror with yet another image as dark and grim as the last one. "What if I can't pay my rent?" "What if I can't find another job?" "What if I lose…" "What if…"

"What If…" surrounds you on all sides with horrifying images of gloom-and-doom. "I'm not qualified for any other job." "There are no jobs out there." "No one is going to hire me." I will lose everything…" You become like someone standing in a Hall of Mirrors who cannot distinguish the true image from all the false ones—they *all* look believable!

All you can envision is the same repetitive outcome—your destruction. Just like in a Hall of Mirrors—it is the *same mirror image* duplicated over and over and over. "What If…" replicates the fatalism in your mind over and over. That is *all* you can think of.

This relentless torment is coming out of your vivid imagination. This is how the spiritual Hall of Mirrors works: your imagination conjures the image that you most dread. Then, Fear projects that image onto mirrors in your mind. From where does Fear get these images? From you! *You* determine the scenarios that threaten your peace.

When you give Me a loaf of bread and a few fish, I multiply that. When you give Fear a dreaded image, he multiplies *that*.

Here is how you escape the Hall of Mirrors: *stop looking in the mirrors!* Anytime you are looking in these mental mirrors, you are looking at the weaknesses inside *yourself*—*your* lack of strength, *your* lack of skills, *your* lack of youthfulness, *your* limited resources.

Instead, close your eyes and re-direct your imagination to recalling *My* strength, *My* skill, and *My* resources. Recall how often you have seen *Me* encompassing you in the past, meeting your every need. You already know that the Hall of Mirrors is not real—it is a magic trick, a terrifying House of Horror. *Stop looking at it!*

THEREFORE, based on what God told me above, the seventh thing we can do to stop the madness of "What If…" is to tell ourselves over and over—until we *believe* it—that these mental images are so horrifying because they are wildly *distorted*. They operate by exaggerating illusions and blurring the truth. Once we recognize that these satanic torments are not real, they lose their power over us because we can then control them.

One negative scenario, of course, would not send us plummeting into despair. We can all handle *one* setback. What our mind *cannot* handle is *all* the imaginary extremes simultaneously. Therefore, to make us feel helpless, "What If…" overloads us with *multiple* stressful scenarios all at once. The truth is, no matter *how* our circumstance is ultimately resolved, it will be resolved in only *one* way—not in the myriad of dreaded ways flashing in our thoughts.

This contrast in outcomes—"one" versus "myriads"—exposes the human weakness that makes us so vulnerable to "What If…" We succumb to Fear because we want to feel in control of *all* the possible outcomes. Humans generally only feel safe when we feel in control.

Our need to always be in control and "prepared for everything" is what Satan feeds on. He creeps into our thoughts by entering through our desperate longing to know the future, to never be caught off-guard, and to want guarantees in life. In our desperation to know how our circumstance will end, we open the door through which Satan enters our vivid imagination. We only invite more impossibilities into a situation that already feels impossible.

THEREFORE, the eighth thing we can do to end "What If…" is to control our need to control things. We will never see into the future. *God*, alone, sees into the future. Only God. "What If…" is simply guesswork. It is the fruit of Satan overfertilizing our imagination.

This is not to say that the unknown cannot be threatening sometimes. I have a history of unemployment to prove it is so. However, there is an upside here for spiritual growth in that we can actually *benefit* from "What If…" If spiritual maturity is truly the end goal of our life on earth, then "What If…" can spotlight the area(s) of our life that we have not yet surrendered to God—areas that remain easy targets for Satan.

That same morning in prayer, God taught me how to *avoid* "What If…"

> Does the thought of unemployment, per se, overwhelm you? No. If that were all you had to worry about, you could deal with that one thing.
>
> You *know* that you have saved money for this very possibility. Of course, if you were *relying* on your savings, Fear would then cause you to start panicking, "What if I don't have *enough* saved?"
>
> But Fear cannot torment you with the thought of not having enough money. Why? Because when it comes to money, you have long relinquished the responsibility for that area of your life to Me. Fear can only torment you with the things that you still feel the need to control.
>
> You only feel overwhelmed when you feel like you are losing control. Conversely, you *cannot* feel overwhelmed by something that is "not your problem." Look at the areas of your life where you have *already* surrendered control to Me:
>
> - Your sales quotas……not your problem.
> - Your retirement income……not your problem.
> - Your savings……not your problem.
> - Your book sales……not your problem.
>
> Why are you not overwhelmed by worries of money when that is what *most* unemployed people would worry about? Because you have grown to trust Me to send you the money you need. Similarly, why can Fear not overwhelm you

with concerns of old age and retirement security? Because you trust Me to somehow sustain you when that time comes.

Fear cannot torment you with the things that you trust Me to provide. However, you panic now because these are areas of your life that you have *not* yet surrendered to Me:

- Where would you live IF... you think *that* is "your problem."
- Who would hire someone your age IF... you think *that* is "your problem."
- Where would you find another job IF... you think *that*, too, is "your problem."

The things that you trust *Me* to handle, Fear cannot use against you. When you trust Me to handle something, you relinquish the responsibility for its outcome to Me. As long as you do not feel responsible for the outcome, Fear cannot threaten you with the outcome. Demons can only exaggerate and distort outcomes that you take on as "your problem." The Hall of Mirrors is more a reflection of *you* than it is of reality.

Conscious thoughts of Me will open an escape route from the Hall of Mirrors. Your awareness of *Me* standing on all sides of you will transport you out of that mental trap and back to reality. And the reality is that *I am God*. I am powerful enough that *all* of your problems can be "not your problem."

THEREFORE, the ninth thing we can do to end "What If..." is to delegate the outcome of our situation to God. This is not the same thing as "not caring" what happens. God admonished me once that "not caring" is *not* the same thing as faith. "Not caring" is when we feel so hopeless that we no longer care *what* Satan does to us. Faith is when we *do* care; we simply view the outcome as "God's problem."

"What If…" and the End Times

I suggested earlier that the purpose of "What If…" is to keep us *feeling* so abandoned, *feeling* so helpless, and *feeling* so hopeless that we *feel* God does not care what happens to us. Of course, God does care. The fact that we are still here is proof that none of the things we thought would "kill us" was allowed to do so. God has always come through, opened a way, parted the sea, and lifted us up out of our circumstances. We have all exhaled that big sigh of relief every time God has proven over again that He *is* the good Father whom He claims to be.

Satan, through his constant harassment and tormenting, however, has been eroding man's confidence in God as the good Father since the beginning of time. In fact, he has been so successful at it that the majority of people—70 percent in a recent poll where I live—do not practice any religion at all. They see no reason to rely on God. Even Christians have been observed subscribing to the propaganda of the world that preaches, "It's every man for *himself.*" "If you want something done right, *you* have to do it *yourself.*" "Pull *yourself* up by the bootstraps."

The Bible has warned us that this day was coming. We simply do not have faith in the Bible either. But it is there—Luke 18:8—"When the Son of Man returns, will He find any faith on earth?"

At the rate in which faith in God is eroding in our churches, I question how much bloodshed will actually be necessary for the Antichrist to ascend to power and rule earth in the End Times. People who have long given up on God will *welcome* someone who shows up with the immediate answer to all their needs and wants. The Antichrist will deceive many people by appearing on the scene as man's "answer to prayer."

All the money we want, all the sex we want, and all the power we want—whenever we want it. The people who have hurt us will "pay." We will get even with anyone who has ever wronged us. Satanism appeals to people in our age precisely because its benefits can be experienced immediately. No waiting. No hold time. No worry. There is no "What If…" for those who follow Satan—he leaves no doubt at all that our every wish and our every grudge will be satisfied instantaneously.

The "problem" is the waiting. God makes us *wait* for our breakthrough. In our society, *"wait"* is a four-letter word! Fast food is never fast enough. Instant rice takes six agonizing minutes to cook. Satan never makes people wait. His kingdom is founded on the promise of instant gratification.

God, of course, intends all along to provide for all of our needs. "All" is the essence of His nature. I used to question why, if God intends all along to give us what we need, does He not simply give it to us. Why put us through the anguish of waiting?

God tests us in waiting because that is how faith is built. We practice faith by trusting and standing on promises that have not yet materialized. We practice faith by resisting the doubt and fear that accompany "What If…" Satan, of course, wants to eradicate faith. His campaign platform is "Why wait when you can have it all now?" By eliminating the wait, Satan is methodically eliminating people's faith.

"What If…" undermines our faith in God by constantly tempting us to doubt God's trustworthiness. When the Antichrist makes his appearance, he will find faith in God almost nonexistent on earth. People's faith will have atrophied from the lack having been exercised. Men will have become like cripples from having lived in perpetual distrust of God's trustworthiness. They will be reluctant to stand behind Someone whose loyalty has always been in question for them. A lifelong "habit" of distrusting God will have so crippled their ability to stand for Him that, in the End Times, they will fall for the propaganda of the Antichrist.

Those who have never learned to silence "What If…" in the fire of trial will fall to the wayside as the heat rises. They will have never endured the flames with enough determination to be forged into the strongest spiritual steel. They will have wasted opportunity upon opportunity on earth, never having learned that to be *tested* by God means to be *strengthened* by God.

Therefore,

when you are being tormented by "What If…," you must:

1. get control of yourself, and harness your wild imagination.
2. stop running from person-to-person, seeking pity.
3. *force* yourself to trust that God has already prepared for this crisis.
4. take breaks to clear your head.
5. unplug the microphone. Literally, command the thoughts to stop.
6. ask God for a sign of His presence.
7. remind yourself that these fears are exaggerated. They are not reality.
8. stop straining to know the future.
9. delegate the outcome to God as "His problem."

MENTAL

Prayer Against

"What If…"

In the authority I have as a child of God,
I *command* you, spirit of Fear:
Get out of my mind!
You and all of your roots, groupings, and familial spirits;
all of your companion, related and interlocking spirits;
you *must* leave now, together as a group.
My future is in *God's* hands!
You can no longer torment me with doubts of His Goodness.
I *cancel* the power of "What If…"
to control, direct, and influence my trust in God,
and I *command* you to leave.
I *forbid* you from communicating with other spirits;
from seeking outside assistance; and
from ever returning.
And, God, I ask Your forgiveness for the times
I believed Satan's threats over Your promises.
I choose to trust in You now.
Amen.

CHAPTER 3

The

Mental Torment

of

Second-Guessing

Second-Guessing

What is Second-Guessing?

Second-Guessing is a mind game that Satan plays on us *after* we have made a good decision. Second-Guessing is a mental torment that causes us to doubt a decision with which, originally, we were confident. It is a ploy that Satan uses to cause us to digress from what the Spirit is leading us to do.

Second-Guessing has characteristics similar to a gambling addiction. Its victims are tormented with nagging thoughts that some big break, some better choice, or some bigger prize may be just around the corner. The result is that we become confused and unsure about *what* we should do. Second-Guessing will sound something like "I'm not sure anymore." "How do I *know* that was really God?" "If only I could know for sure…" The end result of Second-Guessing is always the same: we become immobilized. We end up right where Satan wants us: doing nothing, becoming nothing, and achieving nothing.

But…

Second-Guessing, some people argue, is simply someone trying to be sure. Double-checking—*just to make sure*—does not mean that we are possessed by the devil. Scientists double-check and re-run their experiments all the time as a conclusive way of proving their hypotheses. The world argues that Second-Guessing is actually a prudent way to live. "Making sure" is how we live without regrets. They make a good argument. It just is not true. If it were true, by now—at my age—I should have met at least one person who has lived with no regrets at all.

Fortunately, there *are* distinct differences between human "double-checking" and demonic Second-Guessing that can help us distinguish the two.

How to Recognize Satan

The first way we can recognize Satan is by the unnatural duplicity. In the normal course of our lives, we do not do things twice. No one brushes their teeth twice in the morning. We do not drive to work, then return home, only to drive back to work a second time—unless something is *wrong*. We transact our daily affairs, generally, only once each. When we catch ourselves re-thinking a decision that has already been decided, we must question what would cause us to do something so unnatural.

When we catch ourselves—once again—duplicating the same debate from the beginning, and rehashing the same pros and cons that we have already thoroughly explored, we are behaving irrationally. Irrational, obsessive-compulsive, and repetitive—these are red-flag behaviors. When we are wrestling with duplicity, we can be almost certain that we are wrestling with Satan.

The second way we can recognize Satan is by the confusion he brings. He wants us to re-think, regurgitate, and re-hash to the point that we act like children playing Pin the Tail on the Donkey. Children get spun around to the point that they become too dizzy to put one foot in front of the other. Instead, they wobble and fall to the wayside, missing their mark every time.

This mental dizziness is a trademark of Second-Guessing. Whereas the Holy Spirit will hover over chaos to bring order, the unholy spirits will hover over a situation to *keep* it in confusion. We have all found ourselves in that predicament before: so mentally burned and turned around that we "cannot think straight."

The third way we can recognize Satan is by the torment. If God were "correcting" our wrong decision, He could simply lead us back to the right one. God does not put us through stress-inducing, re-hashing uncertainty. God does not torment us. God does not want us bogged down and shackled in place; He came to bring us the grace and freedom to move on. Even when we do make bad choices, God *convicts* us. He never *torments* us. Only Satan torments and paralyzes.

A fourth way we can recognize that we are wrestling with Satan is by our body's involuntary reaction. We may not know what Satan *looks* like or *sounds* like, but we *can* recognize him by what his presence *feels* like. We can recognize his presence by observing what our physical body is doing. Satan's presence produces feelings of an upset stomach, tension in the chest, headaches, and/or physical exhaustion in the body. We experience sleepless nights. We feel under immense pressure. Short of any objective, causational factors, these are bodily symptoms we experience when our spirit is trying to catch our attention. Things are "not right" when our body starts acting out.

Peace has always been my confirmation when I am in God's will. It just "feels right." That joy in my spirit, that light-heartedness in my chest, that clarity in my thinking—these are all confirmations that I am doing what God is asking of me at that moment. Let us never fall for Satan's lie that we cannot grasp the spiritual realm just because we cannot see it. We can *feel* it!

Satan would only play this game on us if we *had* originally made the right decision. Had we made the *wrong* decision, he would have gladly left us alone. The last thing Satan wants is to steer us back to the right decision. It is not normal for us to be confident one minute and sucked into a vortex of Second-Guessing the next minute over the same decision. Rather than getting sucked in, we can resist Second-Guessing by regaining our original confidence.

On a practical level, regaining our confidence would be similar to an exercise that my friend, a former psychiatric nurse, would assign to couples struggling in their marriage. These couples were Second-Guessing their original decision to have married each other. Satan has a way of taking over the wheel and driving the whole marriage—the baby with the bathwater—over the cliff. And he *will* if we do not regain control of the steering wheel.

My friend would suggest that the couple pull out their wedding photo album. They were told to slowly look through the photos, recalling and sharing what they were *feeling* at the time each photograph was taken. They were instructed to *allow themselves* to re-member, re-call, and re-live the loving emotions and thoughts of those original moments.

The goal of that exercise was to reactivate—to actively experience once again—what had originally made them fall in love with each other. That exercise was often enough for the burned-out couple to remember the love, and to remain standing in their marriage. The couples, of course, still had to work on their commitment, but this "active remembering" exercise often infused them with the rekindled strength and determination to do so.

Restoring our original feelings of enthusiasm—about anything—can be very empowering. We can experience a resurgence of our original dauntless and invincible confidence. Second-Guessing has a way of robbing us of our confidence. The way we counter Second-Guessing is by re-claiming—by taking back—our original confidence. We, like the married couples, put forth the effort to re-member, re-call and re-experience our original enthusiasm.

THEREFORE, the first thing we can do to stop Second-Guessing is to consciously reactivate our original confidence. We must allow ourselves to re-live and re-feel the positive, secure confidence that we originally felt. Placing ourselves emotionally, physically, and mentally back where we felt at *peace* with our decision will force Second-Guessing out of our minds. We cannot both feel at peace and feel uncertain at the same time. Second-Guessing will have to leave.

Once we have made a good decision and have committed ourselves to it, we feel good about it. Inner peace is one of the ways we can always tell when we are aligned with God's will. Our mind relaxes once a matter has been settled. We feel confident moving forward. In our spirit, we *feel* anticipation, not agitation. When we find ourselves repeatedly looking *back* at a settled decision—and *losing* confidence—*that* is a red flag. *That* is Second-Guessing!

THEREFORE, the second thing we can do to stop Second-Guessing is to *force* ourselves to keep looking forward. *STOP LOOKING BACK!* We must resist Satan's rear-view distractions and fix our sight on the optimistic possibilities that are *ahead* of us. We need to consciously turn our thoughts to the *positive* possibilities that await us. Let the rear-view scenery of Second-Guessing disappear from sight.

It is impossible for us to drive straight ahead if we are not looking at the road in front of us.

The Purpose of Second-Guessing

The purpose of Second-Guessing is to steer us out of God's will. Whatever decision we have made—whatever we have decided to do—Satan wants to stop us. There is only one reason why Satan would want to stop us: he feels threatened. While Satan may *resent* our being in God's will, he feels *threatened* when we are actually on the verge of somehow advancing in it.

By the time Satan employs Second-Guessing, he has already lost the first major battle. He could not stop us from *making* the right decision. His back-up plan, then, is to get us to believe that we made a mistake, and reverse our decision. In short, Satan wants us to lose our confidence that it was God and the Holy Spirit who led us to our decision.

Faith is simply the Christian synonym for confidence. When we say that we have *faith* in God, we are saying that we have *confidence* in God. Faith is more than merely a belief that God exists. It is an inner *trust*—unique to Christians—that God is always guiding and coaching us. Faith is Christian trust in God that cannot be scientifically proven; therefore, the world does not trust it.

If Satan could rob us of this one thing—our confident trust in God—he could eliminate Christianity from the world overnight. Second-Guessing is one of the ways he attempts to do this. Second-Guessing is designed to keep us hesitant—unsure that it is God guiding us.

THEREFORE, the third thing we can do to counter Second-Guessing is to keep reaffirming—out loud if necessary—our trust that God would not have led us to the wrong choice. We can boost our trust—our faith—by telling ourselves, over and over, that God has a vested interest in our lives. He would never sit idly by, uninterested in our decisions.

Once God leads us to a decision, we need to stand on it. The book of Ephesians instructs us to do all that our duty requires, and then *stand*. We are to pray, weigh our options, and plan responsibly. Once we have done our reasonable, human part, we are to stand—*to trust*—that God led us to that decision. We cannot waver. To second-guess our decision is to second-guess God. And that is exactly what Satan is hoping we will do. Second-Guessing aims to lure us away from the direction that God has pointed us.

Not knowing is one thing. But Second-Guessing is something else. Second-Guessing is a temptation to sin in that it only comes into play *after* God has already revealed His will to our inner spirit. By the time Satan starts tormenting us with Second-Guessing, we *already* know what we are supposed to do. We felt it earlier in our "gut." We felt at peace with our decision. Our enthusiasm and outlook on life had spiked with confidence.

GO WITH YOUR GUT

Back in grade school, right before we were to take a big, standardized test, one of my teachers gave our class advice on how to improve our test scores. She told us that we will sometimes find ourselves torn between two answers—two choices. We may not be able to decide which choice is the correct one. She suggested that, when in doubt, we should go with our initial gut reaction. She told us that our first instinct is usually the correct one.

This same wisdom applies to life decisions. A real-life example was my decision several months back to schedule vacation time from my job to work on this book. I was so *excited* about my time off. Well, at first...

Just the thought of spending a whole week writing *energized* me. Well, at first...

Literally, as soon as I scheduled my vacation, my sales at work plummeted. Some of my previous sales cancelled. I quickly fell behind my coworkers on the scoreboard. I got called into the office. I had a target on my back. They would be monitoring my performance. And I started Second-Guessing...

Maybe this was not the most prudent time to take off work. Maybe I should use that week instead to catch up on my sales. Satan

MENTAL

began tormenting me with everything "responsible" I should be doing *instead* of writing this book about him.

I took my decision back to prayer. By momentarily falling into the trap of Second-Guessing, I had started doubting that it was God who had inspired me to devote that time to the book. Second-Guessing is a tactic Satan uses to get us to doubt. Doubt ourselves. Doubt God. Doubt what we are doing. Satan loves to drive us to doubt in general because the deeper we slip into the shadow of doubt, the further away we drift from the light of faith.

GOD, IS THIS YOU?

"Lord," I cried, "I have scheduled next week off to work on Your book. Now, I am doubting myself. It is not prudent for me to take off of work when I have fallen so far behind on my sales. Lord, please tell me that You will provide for my sales! You know what I need to stay employed here! This morning I'm so confused that I can't even concentrate!" And God answered...

> Your mind is scattered now; it's true. You are scattered because you are Second-Guessing today, a decision that was made yesterday. Second-Guessing is trying to scare you into changing your mind and choosing the wrong option. You *asked* Me, and I *answered*. But you haven't stopped Second-Guessing since.
>
> Satan always wants you to do the opposite of what I want you to do. Yesterday, I answered YES, so, today, he wants you to think NO. And this is tormenting you. Who would torment you, except Satan?
>
> My responses are swift and direct. Your spirit recognizes My Spirit when He speaks to you. You asked Me about taking off, and I immediately said YES. Fast. Swift. Direct. That is biblical. Was Daniel not assured that as soon as he

prayed, his prayer was answered? That is still how I operate today.

Satan's modus operandi is the exact opposite. Satan drags indecision out as long as possible. He does not *settle* anything in your mind because he wants confusion to reign. You can always recognize Satan's presence by the lack of clarity.

Satan also wants to undermine our relationship. He wants to drive a wedge between us. One way to do this is to cause you to doubt. Doubt that I *answered* you. Doubt that you *heard* Me. If he can get you to doubt that you can trust Me to guide you through life, then he can dismantle your faith in Me. What is faith if not simply another word for *trust*?

Satan wants to destroy your faith in Me by destroying your trust in Me. The goal of Second-Guessing is to cause you to question, to doubt, and to disregard My counsel. He wants you to believe that I do not speak to you. He wants you to believe that when I *do* speak, what you "hear" is not Me.

He is telling you that maybe you just "made that up." Maybe you only heard what you "*wanted* to hear." That maybe you did not think about it long enough.

He wants you to believe that I am vague rather than exact. That I delay rather than answer swiftly. That I am evasive rather than definite and specific.

Every one of these accusations contradicts My Word. I have promised that if you ask, you shall receive. Seek, and you shall find. Knock, and it will be opened for you. This is My Word, and I stand by My Word.

MENTAL

I am not the one causing you to doubt your decision. I *thank* you for turning your cares and concerns over to Me. I *reward* your obedience by giving you the *right answer. Ask* Me, first, to guide your decision-making. Then *act* on what you are prompted to do. Finally, stand firm in that decision.

Satan is the Father of Lies. This is how you can always recognize him—he speaks lies. So, let us right now confront the lies he is whispering in your head…

You *know* that you did not hear wrong because the answer did not come out of "you."

You *know* that it was Me who inspired your decision because it was to Me that you were directing your question at the time.

You *know* that you did not "make up" that answer because, at the time you asked, you were in open-minded, *seeking* mode, not self-sufficient, "I've already decided" mode.

You *know* that you did not imagine only what you "wanted to hear" because, at the time you asked, your mind was fully open to *whatever* answer I might have given you.

Armed with all these things you *know* about your decision, you have no reason to be Second-Guessing. The only reason you are Second-Guessing is because Satan is planting doubt in your mind.

Satan will immediately rush in after you have made a right decision to get you to reverse it. He must move quickly before you act on it. Afterall, *his* plan for you is that you never accomplish *My* plan for you.

Satan wants you Second-Guessing the calling I have for your life because if you lose your confidence, you will lose your determination to do it. When you are Second-Guessing, everything shuts down. All of your forward progress ceases. Everything is in limbo. You mentally tread water, exhausting yourself in uncertainty, and getting nowhere.

THEREFORE, based on what God told me above, the fourth thing we can do to stop Second-Guessing is to remind ourselves of what we *know* about how we arrived at our original decision. This is important because what is *true,* is of God. We did not arrive at our original decision willy-nilly. In fact, we ourselves did not make that decision. It was *God* who planted the proclivity—the answer—in our gut; we just went along with it. The matter was originally settled *that* way. Now is not the time to start doubting how God works with us.

When we take the stress of decision-making upon ourselves, we are usurping God's role. How can we presume to know the effect of today's decision on our life ten years down the road? Only God can see that far into the future. No wonder Second-Guessing is so stressful—we are *straining* to know things that are impossible for humans to know!

THEREFORE, the fifth thing we can do to end Second-Guessing is to stop straining so hard to know how the future will play out. If we believe that God *wants* what is good for us, then we must also believe that He is good enough to make it happen. And He *will* make it happen in order to get us to where He needs us positioned. We are not responsible for *making* His decision; we are only responsible for going along with it.

How This Mind Game Works

Second-Guessing works the same way that *all* of Satan's ambushes work: by redirecting our focus away from God and back onto ourselves. Second-Guessing causes us, not to doubt God, but to doubt ourselves. The efficacy of Second-Guessing lies in its ability to keep our focus off of God's resources, and stuck on our *lack* of resources.

Second-Guessing generates thoughts that God is not actively involved in our lives. God may speak to *some* people, but *we* cannot hear Him. God *is* with mankind in theory, but *we* cannot see Him. The Holy Spirit is *constantly* nudging other people, but *we* cannot know for sure that it is Him. And, if we "feel" something, that was probably "just me."

The success of Second-Guessing depends on its ability to convince us that we are too ordinary to be doing spiritual things. We are too imperfect to be led by the Spirit. We are definitely too unimportant to receive God's personalized attention. I shudder to think of how few miracles the apostles would have performed on earth if they had first stopped to second-guess if it was God—or just their imaginations—prompting them to lay hands on people. The Bible today would be a very thin book.

Second-Guessing and the End Times

Second-Guessing operates in our lives to form a *pattern* of hesitating, reconsidering, and doubting when God calls us to do something. This mental torment chips away at our confidence to recognize God's voice and to respond confidently to His promptings. Satan hopes that eventually we will become like children who simply dismiss and ignore their parents. Satan's goal is to establish a *habit* of our rethinking and reevaluating everything, even things that have been settled. By never allowing the dust to settle, Satan causes us to live in fogginess rather than clarity, and uncertainty rather than boldness.

Earlier in this chapter, I proposed that the purpose of Second-Guessing is to steer us out of God's will. By the time the Antichrist appears, Satan will have had *centuries* of practice wearing down our obedience, our confidence, and our boldness. We will have grown so sluggish in responding to the promptings of the Holy Spirit that we will find ourselves watching the heavenly cloud depart while we remain behind, still making up our mind.

Not responding will be recorded in the Book of Life as our response. In hindsight, the *right* answers will be so painfully obvious. Our earthly failures will rise to the level of denying Christ in that, at the time we hesitated, we *knew* in our gut what we were being led to do. We will have allowed Second-Guessing to steer us, in the end, to not doing it.

I sometimes still experience Second-Guessing causing me to walk out of God's will, assignment, and call to holiness. Of course, my *intentions* are good. I *mean* well. I cannot help the thoughts I wrestle with. I am only human. And I am always sorry afterward. God knows my heart, and He knows I am sorry.

We, like children who have misbehaved but do not want to take their punishment, will plead in the End Times that we are sorry. We will cry, "The devil made me do it!" This, of course, will be true. It was true back when Eve said it, too, but that did not absolve her of her punishment. The "good" criminal also had a change of heart up on that hill—he, too, was sorry—but he still had to die a torturous death on that cross for the poor choice he had made earlier. Using Satan as the excuse for all that we have done—and all that we have failed to do—will not relieve us of accountability either.

In the End Times, when all our institutions have collapsed, our governments have fallen, and violence and human sacrifice are rampant, all that will remain for Christians is that small, inner voice of the Spirit which Second-Guessing has worked our entire lifetime to drown out. God, of course, will be with us until the end of time. God will do what He has *always* done for us: empower us, counsel us, and reveal the way to us. It is my belief that so many of us believers will be deceived by the Antichrist because we, too, will be doing what *we* have always done: Second-Guessing.

Therefore,

when you are being tormented by Second-Guessing, you must:

1. reinstate—*re-fill*—yourself with your original feeling of confidence.
2. stop looking back. Focus on looking forward.
3. remind yourself that God has not abandoned you.
4. review how you *know* God was behind your original decision.
5. trust God to know the future, and just go along with His decision.

MENTAL

Prayer Against

Second-Guessing

In the authority I have as a Christian,
I *declare* my dominion over you, spirit of Doubt!
I *order* you to remove yourself—
with all of your roots, groupings, and familial spirits;
all of your companion, related and interlocking spirits—
from my peace and clear thinking.
I *command* that you can no longer
poison my confidence or
disturb my faith in God with Second-Guessing.
No longer can you cause me to hesitate or delay.
I *command* you to leave my mind.
I *forbid* you from communicating with other spirits,
from seeking outside assistance, and
from ever returning.
Father, I ask Your forgiveness for taking my eyes off You,
and for allowing Satan to temporarily lead me astray.
Restore my confidence, I pray,
so that I can follow without hesitation
the direction in which You are pointing me.
Amen.

CHAPTER 4

The

Mental Torment

of

Splitting Hairs

Splitting Hairs

What is Splitting Hairs?

Splitting Hairs is a demonic, word-twisting game born out of our conversations with other people. It is a nit-picking, pick-apart torment of syntax. Splitting Hairs lures us into thinking too hard, too long, and too suspiciously about things people have said. It plants the thought in our head that there are ulterior motives and implications behind what people have actually said. The more we pick apart their words, the more we are sure to find the ulterior motives we set out to find. Satan first played this game on Adam and Eve.

In the garden of Eden, Adam and Eve were originally very happy. Sin had never crossed their minds because they had no reason to sin. There was no human desire, no human longing that was not already being met. Adam and Eve certainly *knew* about the tree of Knowledge of Good and Evil. They could *see* it. God had not hidden it from them. They simply had no reason to eat of its fruit. There was no human appetite of theirs that was not already being satisfied. They had never sinned before because there was nothing to be gained from sinning. So, why did they sin? Let us pause for a moment and think about this…

…And that was where they went wrong.

This is where we *all* go wrong.

Satan got them to pause for a moment, and start thinking that there were ulterior motives behind what God had said. Satan got them to start thinking too hard, too long, and too suspiciously about God's motivation. Before that infamous day, Adam and Eve had always simply taken God at His word. They took everything God told them at face-value. They took God—*literally*—at His word. When we believe God's Word, there is nothing to "interpret." We have no reason to look for hidden meanings or implied innuendos.

We have no compulsion to search for ulterior motives. There is no temptation to split hairs. Well, unless Satan gets involved.

Splitting Hairs sometimes ensnares me in my relationships with others. Following a conversation—after we have hung up the phone or walked away—the thought comes to me to start nit-picking their words. "Wait, what exactly did she mean by...?" "Hold on, was he insinuating...?" "Now that I think about it, was he trying to say...?" "Why did she say it like that?"

After the conversation is over, and we have parted ways, Splitting Hairs starts twisting their words in my head. Their words start to take on a different meaning the harder I *look* for a different meaning. When I start thinking, "Wait a minute, was she implying..." *that* is Splitting Hairs!

But...

"This is actually a *positive* thing," some people argue. This is a matter of social survival. It is actually a sign of our mental astuteness. When nothing "slips past us" or goes "over our head," they argue, that is proof of our superior mental acuity, not proof of some imaginary little man dressed in red and holding a pitch fork.

In this cut-throat, dog-eat-dog world we live in, they argue, we need to know who our friends are. Despite the fact that we all say we do not care what others think about us, we all *do* care. And there is no better way to gauge what people think of us than by their own words.

None of us wants to invest ourselves in people who do not have our back. We need a way to distinguish the people who *have* our back from the people *stabbing* us in the back. Dissecting people's words is how we weed out our enemies; it has nothing to do with Satan. They do make a good argument. Their argument, however, simply ignores all of the rational reasons that *contradict* their argument.

How to Recognize Satan

The first way we know that Satan is involved is by the unnatural behavior of the people around us. Of course, we all know people who *are* insulting, demeaning, and critical. They only half-heartedly hide behind the sarcasm they think flies "over our head." When we see these people approaching, we brace ourselves for another caustic encounter. Experience has trained us to *expect* something critical from them.

What is *unnatural*, however, is for our friends to say hurtful things to us. It is *unnatural* for the people in our prayer group to be sarcastic with us. When our natural, routine interactions with people suddenly become unnatural, irregular, and out of character—*that* is a red flag. Something is "not right." Something unnatural is going on. Something unnatural has interjected itself into our routine human interactions. That unnatural "something" is Satan.

A second way we can recognize Satan is by our *own* unnatural behavior. "Why am I doing this?" Any rational person would have to ask themselves this question. It is unnatural for us to go back, after the fact, and scramble sentences to mean something different than we understood them to mean at the time they were spoken.

If the other person had truly said something offensive or critical, we certainly would have caught it at the time. We would have been offended back then, on the spot. We are not stupid. There is no "jet lag" in our understanding conversation. We do not typically have to wait thirty minutes to understand someone's statement. This is not natural human behavior.

The third way we know that Splitting Hairs is satanic is by its inconsistency. If we were naturally people who over-think—people who naturally dissect, and nit-pick words—we would do this with *all* our conversations. We would subject *compliments* to the same nit-picking, cynical process that we do insults. But this is not what we do. No one does this because this is not normal behavior. This is simply not "how we are." This is Satan.

The fourth way we can recognize Satan's interference is by the illogical results. One of the contradictions of Splitting Hairs is that, under the guise of discovering the truth, the truth is rarely found. Splitting Hairs yields results that are not objective. Every time we nit-pick people's words, we *always* find a slight or insult. We *never* find something flattering or uplifting. It is a mathematical impossibility that our searches would *always* yield negative results.

This is no coincidence. It defies logic that *every single time* we dissect words we find a motive that is negative. If Splitting Hairs was truly about uncovering the truth, as some people argue, it would yield negative results *some* of the time, positive results *some* of the time, and neutral results *some* of the time. But it does not. The results are *always* negative.

The fifth way we can recognize Satan is by the compulsive behavior he incites. When we are caught up in Splitting Hairs, we find ourselves spending an unnatural amount of time and energy doing it. It is like an addictive video game: we cannot put it down. We *cannot stop* thinking about what that person said. We cannot let it go. We are compelled to mull it over, examining and dissecting their every word from every conceivable angle. The amount of time that we dedicate to Splitting Hairs each day is out of proportion with our true priorities in life.

Splitting Hairs will cause us to waste an inordinate amount of our time—precious time that could be spent doing something productive. I personally resent days that I have wasted doing "nothing" and getting "nothing" accomplished. It is time "well spent" only to Satan because it is time spent destroying, dividing, and distancing us from the body of Christ.

THEREFORE, the first thing we can do to defeat Splitting Hairs is to force ourselves to do something else, something productive. Stop *thinking* and go *do!* Get the clothes washed. Clear all those papers off the kitchen table. Plant some flowers.

Pitting people against each other is a priority of Satan's agenda. Splitting Hairs diverts our natural inclination from bonding *with* people to bracing *against* people. Satan must keep us at odds with each other because *anytime* Christians unite, it is always to oppose evil. Discord, Division, and Distrust are the names of actual demons. These spirits are not of God. When we find ourselves behaving in unison with these dark forces, Satan has already found his way into our thoughts.

THEREFORE, the second thing we can do to stop Splitting Hairs is to intentionally think the *opposite* of what Satan wants us to think. When Splitting Hairs tempts us to dwell on how that person *may* have insulted us, we should dwell instead on how that person has been *kind* to us in the past. This has a cancelling effect on the negativity. This has a healing effect on the rift. This has a strengthening impact on the friendship. This is how, in practical terms, we resist Satan. We exert energy in the opposite direction that he is pushing us.

The fruit of Splitting Hairs is that we become defensive and guarded—the opposite of being open and inclusive. We very quickly erect protective barriers between us and others. We distance ourselves from people. We stiffen up and declare that no one will ever get close enough to ever hurt us again. We live cynical and "ready" for the next blow, even if there was never a blow in the first place.

THEREFORE, the third thing we can do to stop Splitting Hairs is to immediately give that person the benefit of the doubt. We blame Satan for the negative thoughts we get after the fact, not the other person. Extending the benefit of the doubt to others is not merely a noble Christian virtue; it is practical, hands-on, everyday spiritual warfare.

The Purpose of Splitting Hairs

The purpose of Splitting Hairs is to divide people—to pit us against each other. Splitting Hairs always undermines unity. Satan keeps us fighting and biting each other by using enflaming thoughts that arouse division, indignation, and discord. The result of Satan's Splitting Hairs is that it prevents us from uniting together to fight *him!*

By twisting the words of others, Satan gets us thinking that *people* are our enemy, rather than him. As long as Satan can keep our focus on *people*, he can remain safely out of our crosshairs. The veil that separates the human realm from the spiritual realm is so very thin that Satan,to avoid being exposed, must keep us distracted and intensely preoccupied with *people.*

Splitting Hairs keeps us thinking that we "missed it" the first time. The problem or "delay" is with us. This is so typical of Satan. Blame others. Blame yourself. Blame *anybody* except him. The truth is, we did not "miss something" earlier. We understood what was being said at the time it was said. We only further Satan's agenda when we blame ourselves.

"It takes me a while to catch on." No, it does not. We understood—and accepted—what the other person said at the time. We are not "just now" understanding the conversation. We are *not* just now "catching on"—we are actually just now Splitting Hairs!

"But now that I'm thinking about it..." No, we are not now thinking about "it"—about what they said. Now, just like he did with Adam and Eve, Satan does not have us thinking about the *words,* but rather, *guessing* about ulterior motives that were *not* said. *That* is the reason we are "now" thinking—we are now *looking* for ulterior motives.

"Come to think about it..." This is a lie. This implies that we have *just now* reached the point of thinking about it—for the first time. But we are *not* just now "coming" to think about it; we thought about it earlier when it was first spoken. We are not *coming* to think about it, but, rather, going *back* to think about it. Only, this time, with sinister intentions.

"The more I think about it..." This too is a lie. The truth is, we are *not* thinking "more" about what *was said*. We are not *continuing* to think about the same earlier conversation. Rather, we are thinking about something *new!* We are just now—*for the first time*—thinking that the conversation was actually saying something different—something negative. This is a *new* conversation that we are entertaining. Splitting Hairs is *replacing* the "old" conversation with this "new" conversation that has been spun by Satan.

THEREFORE, the fourth thing we can do to stop Splitting Hairs is refuse to get sucked into this bizarre, twisted game. The same way we choose to not participate in adultery, to not participate in drunkenness, to not participate in illegal drug use, etc., so, too, do we choose to *not* participate in twisted, re-constructed conversations *JUST SAY NO!* We can simply *refuse* to "go there." By refusing to re-invent and re-create conversations, we defeat Satan.

Words carry power. This is why human words have always been so important to a spiritual being like Satan. As soon as God created man, Satan rushed to destroy us using words. Not lust, not greed, not envy—but *words* were the cause of Original Sin. This is how Satan has always intended to drive the human race to destroy itself—by twisting words. The following are two real-life, very common examples of how easily we can be deceived by the manipulation of words.

MENTAL

YES OR NO

One of my dear friends once shared with me something that she learned years earlier from one of the old nuns who taught civics at Grand Coteau. The topic that particular day was the American privilege to vote. We routinely vote on amendments, taxes, and ordinances, etc., to tell our lawmakers how we want to be governed. Since most of us are not politicians, activists, or political lobbyists, we often find maneuvering through the nuances and technical wording of legal amendments difficult—not to mention boring.

My friend and her classmates were warned of two common word games that unscrupulous politicians play to manipulate voters. These two examples of trickery illustrate how the manipulation of words can produce the desired, but unethical, result. The first trap is to word the amendment with double negatives. An example of this would be, "It shall not be a crime to not refrain from killing people."

Most voters will see the words *crime* and *kill* in the same sentence, and vote *for* the amendment because we *all* want killing to be a crime! However, the way the amendment is worded with double negatives, the average citizen is tricked into voting to *legalize* killing people!

In my own state of Louisiana, we once had a very wealthy, very prestigious family whose domestic feuds were also very public. Chalin Perez and his second wife battled publicly for two decades with the children from his first marriage. Mr. Perez wanted to make sure that his children did not get any of his assets after his death. It is noteworthy that Mr. Perez's own wealth came out of the very institution he was now opposing: inheritance from one's parents.

Louisiana's forced heirship laws at the time required that community property be passed to one's children upon their death. Mr. Perez's primary asset with his first wife was land. For this reason, moving with his new wife to another state would not accomplish his vendetta. His wealth—the land—could not be moved to another state. As such, the land remained subject to Louisiana's inheritance laws.

Louisiana's forced heirship laws had been in place for centuries, and the people here *wanted* that to be our law. Part of the rationale behind forced heirship was that, upon the death of one's parents, their children should not become the responsibility of the State and rely on welfare. A second rationale for forced heirship was the assurance that, upon one's death, everything the parents had worked to build would remain in their family. No smooth-talking lawyer could steal it out of the hands of their children.

Public opinion was against Mr. Perez, and he knew it. So was the law, and he knew it. He knew that he would never change the heart of the people here. Nor would the people of Louisiana allow him to circumvent the law. His only recourse, then, was to get the law changed.

He hired a lobbyist and "persuaded" our legislators to word a new forced heirship amendment in an unnatural, negative format. Money was no object for him. In October, 1995 his new constitutional amendment on forced heirship was put on the ballot for the common folk to have their voices heard and express their wishes. Well, at least in theory.

I voted *against* that amendment because my friend had already warned me to be skeptical of amendments worded in the negative. That is a game of manipulating words to trick people. So, I voted NO. But I was in the minority. The negatively-worded amendment—no surprise—passed by an overwhelming two-to-one vote.

The aftermath of the vote created a great uproar across the State. People quickly realized that they had been tricked. The majority of voters thought they had voted to *keep* forced heirship. However, because the amendment was worded in the negative, they had been tricked into voting to end it. There was a state-wide effort to demand a re-vote. The people of Louisiana wanted a do-over to correct the deception. But the paid-off politicians would not have it. The people of Louisiana, they claimed, had "spoken."

For the second example of how words can be manipulated to muddle our thinking, we will continue with the old nun's civics lesson. My friend and her classmates were also warned by the old nun to be wary of amendments that are unnaturally long. The old nun's advice echoes the famous Shakespearean line, "Me doth think thou protests too much." The lesson here is that excessive wording—overkill—is often a "red flag" of deception.

If politicians truly want to know the will of the people, they can simply ask. Just ask. Do you want to renew the library tax? Yes or no.

Do you want to widen Main Street to four lanes? Yes or no. Do you want to use the city's slush fund to build a bridge? Yes or no.

Many times, when we are asked to vote on amendments, we are faced with lengthy, multiple-paragraph amendments. These amendments can be so complicated by, not only legal terminology, but also categories and subcategories with references to other Articles and subsections. The lengthy run-on sentences are broken up with so many commas that we forget what the beginning of the sentence was even talking about! When politicians have something to hide, the old nun warned, they bury it in excessive and technical wording. The true meaning of what they want to do becomes lost in the sheer volume of words. The old nun's advice: JUST VOTE NO!

Splitting Hairs works on the same two deceptive principles: negativity and over-kill. The *only* reason Satan gets us re-thinking and nit-picking words after a conversation is to reconstruct them in a negative format. We also get sucked into Splitting Hairs by the overkill—the same words over and over and over. The nit-picking goes on and on and on. Splitting Hairs digresses so far off point that we lose sight of the original intent. Satan uses Splitting Hairs to trick us into making decisions *he* wants us to make. And what Satan wants is discord, discontentment, and distrust within the body of Christ. He wants the eye to snub the hand and the head to disown the feet because he knows that a disjointed body will lack the strength to protect itself.

How This Mind Game Works

Splitting Hairs works like the man in the moon. Never has anyone *looked* for the man in the moon and not found him. We will always find what we set out to find. The longer we stare at the moon, and strain to *find* a nose and two eyes, the more these features emerge. This man's face, of course, is all in our imagination, but once we "see" the man in the moon, we can no longer look at the moon and *not* see him.

To illustrate how Splitting Hairs works, I will repeat a sentence—the exact same sentence—several times. Each time, I will simply strain to focus on a different word in the sentence. My hypothetical example is of a loyal friend who *defended* me when money went missing from the cash register at work. However, by the time Splitting Hairs gets finished planting thoughts in my mind, I am convinced that my best friend is actually my worst enemy!

This is what my hypothetical friend actually said: "I never said you stole money from the company."

Okay, I'm glad she was saying…
I *never* said you stole money from the company.

On second thought, was she saying…
I never said *you* stole money from the company.

But wait, what was she implying when she said…
I never said you stole money from the company.

How dare she say…
I never said you stole *money* from the company.

Originally, I believed that my friend defended my character. She *never* accused me. In the second thought, it starts to sound like she was part of the gossip who accused *someone* of stealing. In the third thought, my friend admits that she *knew* I was the one reported for stealing, but she did nothing to defend me. In the last twisted thought, my "friend" confesses that she *did* report me for stealing something—just not money.

The more time I spend splitting hairs, the deeper the division between us grows. First, Satan re-words her statement in the negative. Secondly, he uses over-kill to churn the words over and over in my mind. By the end of the day, Splitting Hairs has destroyed our friendship (Division). I will hate her for the rest of my life (Discord). I will never speak to her again (Isolation). And I will make sure that all of our mutual friends know what a back-stabber she is (Distrust)! She and I will never again bond together and agree on anything. Satan will have succeeded in his objective that she and I never realize the power of "When two or more are gathered in My name…"

Splitting Hairs and the End Times

The purpose of Splitting Hairs, again, is to divide people—to turn us against each other. Splitting Hairs is employed to undermine unity. This is a well-known military strategy—divide and conquer. Splitting Hairs has an important role to play in the ushering in of the reign of the Antichrist: eliminate every threat of organized resistance.

We are all familiar with 1 Corinthians 12:21 which uses the analogy of body parts to warn us that we will not survive without each other. The church, in order to remain a light to the nations, needs every brick of its lighthouse to remain firmly in place. God, too, needs all of us because He has assigned different spiritual functions to each of us.

When Satan pits us against each other, and friendships are destroyed, we often part ways, thinking, "I don't need her as a friend anyway." People get divorced every day, thinking that they are "better off" alone than with the other. Many of us live in neighborhoods where neighbors expect neighbors to stay on their side of the fence.

We live today like the people of Corinth who needed a lesson in why we should strive to live together. This is not how God intended for us to live—not speaking, not sharing, not forgiving, not bonding. This is how *Satan* intends for us to live. He knows that when we are alone, we are most vulnerable to attack.

There is strength in numbers. We are stronger together because we each have different strengths to contribute to the whole. To paraphrase the famous Aesop's fable, an individual stick, when bundled with other sticks, cannot be broken.

Those apostles hiding in fear of their lives—together, as one body—in the upper room were able to encourage and strengthen each other to remain faithful to Christ. That is what we will need in the End Times when we ourselves will be hiding underground in fear. At that time, many people will be running from door-to-door—even to the doors to our churches—begging to be let in, but their cries will be ignored. The people inside will simply put their hands over their ears to muffle the blood-curdling screams in the streets. That is the thing about the human body: once a foot is cut off, it does not grow back.

Therefore,

when you are being tormented by Splitting Hairs, you must:

1. decide that your time is too valuable to waste on Splitting Hairs. Go do something productive.
2. recall the other person's goodness to you in the past to offset the negativity.
3. give people the benefit of the doubt.
4. make a determined resolution to *not* "go there."

MENTAL

Prayer Against

Splitting Hairs

I *declare* my authority in Christ Jesus
over *you*, spirit of Division;
over your roots, groupings, and familial spirits; and
over your companion, related and interlocking spirits!
Stop recreating and dissecting their words to
create dissention, discord, and division.
I *command* that you can no longer
Nit-pick my thoughts, memories, or recollections.
I *reject* and *retract* the power I have given you,
and I now *command* you to be silent.
I *forbid* you from communicating with other spirits,
from seeking outside assistance, and
from ever returning.
Lord, I now choose to forgive the hurt,
whether real or perceived, involving this person.
Forgive me, too, for any unintentional,
hurtful words I may have spoken to them.
Please erase all thoughts of distrust
from my heart and mind.
Renew in me the joy
of knowing Your friendship and theirs.
Amen.

CHAPTER 5

The

Mental Torment

of

Obsessing

Obsessing

What is Obsessing?

Let me address at the onset of this chapter what spiritual Obsessing is *not*. When we toss and turn all night long, unable to sleep for thinking about the stress at work, that is *not* Obsessing. That is fear—that is lack of faith. When we cannot stop crying, getting angry, and feeling betrayed by an unfaithful spouse, that is *not* Obsessing. That is mourning—pure, raw grief. When we re-live over and over how someone has hurt us, that is *not* Obsessing. That is plain and simple unforgiveness.

Obsessing as used in this book refers to a demonic obstruction that prevents us from finalizing a decision. When we are being controlled by Obsessing, our mind churns constantly over some, often minor, detail ad nauseam. This one minor detail blocks us from committing to a final decision and moving forward. Obsessing leaves our mental torment ongoing with no end in sight. It works very much like someone bracing a door open with their foot, not allowing it to close.

What should be a relatively minor decision becomes blown so far out of proportion and made so complicated that we get trapped in a never-ending, open-ended debate in our head. We simply cannot make a final a decision, put closure, and move on. This is one of the telltale red flags that alerts us to the likelihood of demons influencing our thinking: the nagging inability to put closure.

Obsessing is when we become abnormally paralyzed by a specific detail of a pending decision. Obsessing is a stumbling block that Satan uses to prevent us from bringing one thing to completion so we can move forward to the next thing. Obsessing keeps us perpetually indecisive and uncommitted, scared that we will "get it wrong." Obsessing is when all forward progress in an area of our life comes to a screeching halt because of perpetual indecisiveness.

MARIE HEBERT

THE KITCHEN CABINETS

Years ago, I lived in a small rural town where many of the town's original buildings had been "re-purposed" over the years. Such was the case with the turn-of-the-century two-room schoolhouse next door to our property.

A retired judge and his wife had purchased the property years before we had ever moved there. The renovations had dragged on for years. The carpenter—their son—had already been working for over *ten years* exclusively on their house. That poor man had been forced to re-do the same work over and over multiple times. They always found something wrong with the wood grain, or the corners, or the height, or the...whatever. Their house had to be P.E.R.F.E.C.T.

Eventually, the entire schoolhouse was finally repaired, refinished, and remodeled. The wooden staircase and hardwood floors had all been restored. The grand piano had been delivered. The grounds had been landscaped. All the windows had been replaced. The heating and cooling systems modernized. The plumbing and electrical work had been entirely updated. Every detail was P.E.R.F.E.C.T. Well, everything except the little knobs on the kitchen cabinets. The wife had still not made a final decision on the kitchen cabinet knobs.

The woman was under such pressure to make the P.E.R.F.E.C.T. choice that she could not make any choice at all. She became overwhelmed and totally paralyzed by what, to most people, would have been a simple decision.

In actuality, no one cared about the silly knobs. That one, minute detail, however, held up the finalizing of the renovations. Obsessing had completely paralyzed her. I lived next door to them for thirteen years and moved away before she ever decided on her cabinet knobs. Obsessing had robbed her of *years* of enjoyment.

But...

What I am calling Obsessing, some people argue, is simple human prudence. Careful planning and attention to detail are qualities to be admired. Since when does being detail-oriented mean that we are possessed by the Devil? The skeptics do make a good argument. Their argument is "good," but *not* because it is valid. Their argument is "good" in that it is effective in getting people to downplay the likelihood of Satan's involvement.

Mockery is a very effective tool today in silencing Christians. Ridicule from the world can make us feel foolish. The world does it to us all the time: mock Christian faith and practices in order to discredit and silence us. The condescending sneers and eye-rolling of other's is often all it takes for most of us to back down and bite our tongue—to not draw attention to ourselves.

I would like to point out that there is nothing "prudent" about Obsessing. It is a mental trap that is neither efficient nor admirable. Obsessing is not "working through" a dilemma. In fact, it yields the exact opposite result. Instead of "solving" our dilemma, Obsessing *prolongs* our dilemma!

Our challenge is to recognize the difference between Satan and simple human prudence. Fortunately, there are several characteristics of this mental torment that can identify its satanic origin.

How to Recognize Satan

The first way we can recognize Satan is that Obsessing thoughts are driven and manic. They never stop. They never slow down. They never pause. These thoughts barrel through our minds with the unstoppable force and fury of a runaway train. Obsessing will not stop, even though we want it to stop. Obsessing produces an out-of-control feeling *because* we are no longer the one in control.

The second way we can recognize Satan is that our thinking is grossly exaggerated. Obsessing blows our decisions unrealistically out of proportion. "Once-and-for-all," "for all eternity," "till death do us part," and "written in stone" are *not* characteristics of rational thinking. It would not be cataclysmic, years down the road, for us to change the knobs on our kitchen cabinets. Once trapped inside Obsessing, however, nothing seems to be of more dire consequence than this one little detail.

The third way we can recognize Satan is by the fruit he produces. Being consumed with persistent thoughts, alone, is not conclusive evidence of Satan's involvement. For example, what child does not think persistently about what he hopes Santa will bring Christmas morning? Morning, noon, and night, that is all that child thinks about. That could be considered "obsessing," but it is not satanic.

Looking forward to something we greatly desire is normal. In fact, the fruit of anticipation can be very positive and beneficial. The fruit of Satan, however, is the opposite. Anticipation *energizes* us! Splitting Hairs *drains* us. Therefore, when discerning for satanic activity, we always look at the fruit. If the fruit we harvest is stressful, frustrating, and paralyzing, then it is poisoned by Satan.

The Purpose of Obsessing

The purpose of Obsessing is to prevent us from accomplishing things. To prevent us from moving further along God's plan for us. To prevent us from fulfilling our purpose. The goal of Obsessing is to overwhelm us mentally to the point where we become paralyzed and unable to proceed forward. Obsessing churns and churns relentlessly in order to wear us down. Obsessing consumes all of our energy so that we have no energy or confidence left to actually complete anything.

When Obsessing, we get "stuck" like a needle on a scratched record that plays the same word over and over and over. All we hear, all we think about, all we can focus on is that one detail. We cannot get beyond it. Back in the days of vinyl records this used to happen to me often. My albums would invariably get scratched. When the needle got stuck on a scratch, I would have to walk over to the record player and nudge the needle forward. It was not going to move forward by itself.

MENTAL

IT'S GOTTA BE PERFECT

I, myself, fell into Obsessing as I neared the completion of my very first book years ago. I was so afraid that some reader, someday, somewhere in the world, would find some little grammatical error that I could not give final approval to the manuscript. I needed that book to be P.E.R.F.E.C.T.

The very hallmark of Obsessing is that we are *never* able to put closure. I would spring up in the middle of the night, thinking of where I needed to change a comma to a semicolon. I was constantly juggling and rearranging the same words over and over. My mind could never rest. It was like I was under a spell, and I could not break free. I felt "forced" to keep staring at the same pages over and over.

I stressed over that manuscript for sixteen months (the average turnaround time for the publication of a book is only nine months). I could not stop *looking* for words to improve it, *seeking* words to substitute, *reaching* for words to clarify it, and *digging* for words that were more succinct. I could never reach a point where I felt that the book was "finished." It was a vicious cycle of "Not yet…" "There could be something else I haven't considered…" "Let me just make sure one more time…"

God had to *tell* me that it was Satan. Obsessing was working to delay—or prevent—that book's publication! "JUST STOP!" God admonished me, "STOP NIT-PICKING! It is Satan causing you to spin in circles over the same sentences over and over. Stop trying to create a book that is P.E.R.F.E.C.T."

God told me that my torment was never going to stop unless *I* put a stop to it. I would have to push myself past Satan's roadblock. So, I took a deep breath and made a determined decision that my next edit would be my *last* edit. I revised that book one last time and forced myself to hit the SEND button.

My torment stopped immediately. It *all* stopped. The very instant I hit SEND, I felt like the weight of the whole world had been lifted from my shoulders. It was over! I took a deep breath and exhaled sixteen months of pent-up stress. The unrelenting compulsion was finally over. My torment was over *just that fast.* Just that fast,

Obsessing *stopped*. Why? Because I *forced* myself to move past the indecision and get out of limbo.

Therefore, the first thing we can do when we are trapped in Obsessing is to *force* ourselves to stop. Just stop! It is not rational for us to think that the same options we have been churning over and over are suddenly going to change. They will not. We accomplish nothing by continuing to rehash the same details over and over. Obsessing does not shed any new light or reveal anything new. To break free of Obsessing, we have to *force* ourselves out of it. We must decide that we are *finished thinking* about it—the same way that we demand a final answer from a child who cannot decide on which flavor of ice cream they want. Just stop, and break Satan's spell!

Sometimes, even though we do not like to hear it, we bring Obsessing upon ourselves. In my example of the kitchen cabinets, my neighbor had invited that agony on herself. Yes, Satan *fueled* it, but he had not *caused* it. Her pride had sucked her into that torment. Pride had backed her into a corner, and Obsessing made sure that she never came out of it. She had to *prove* that everything she had, everything she did, and everything she owned was better than what anyone else had, even something as trivial as the knobs on her kitchen cabinets.

Pride was the same flaw that snared me. I wanted to write the P.E.R.F.E.C.T. book. As the completion of that first book neared, that book had become less about promoting *God's* name and more about promoting my own. I wanted to be this great author whom everyone revered and wanted to read. "Vanity of vanities; all is vanity," Shakespeare said—and he was quoting *that* from the Book of Ecclesiastes!

Therefore, the second thing we can do to stop Obsessing is to take an inventory of our hidden motivation. Obsessing feeds on weakness—like a stray cat that, once it finds food, never leaves. If Obsessing is feeding off of our pride, it is better for us to acknowledge it and remove the food dish. If we recognize it, we can stop it. If we recognize it, we have power over it.

It is particularly noteworthy that in both the example of my neighbor's kitchen cabinets and the example of my first book, Obsessing made its appearance right as each of our respective projects was coming to an end. Both the completion of her renovations and the completion of my book marked the end of a phase or "season" for us. The satisfactory completion of that season was necessary for each of us to move into our next season. For my neighbor, that next season was the ministry of hospitality. For myself, the next season was ministry. No wonder Satan had to stop us—we were each preparing to move into some form of service.

THEREFORE, the third thing we can do to break the gridlock of Obsessing is to force ourselves to look forward. Look to what awaits us *beyond* the present roadblock. "Once the kitchen cabinets are finished, we can start inviting people over for coffee!" "My *next* book is going to be about..." By turning our energy future-focused, we break the immobilizing grip of Obsessing. Forward-thinking, forward-dreaming, and forward-looking give us *something else*—something very positive—to focus on. It creates traction—the grabbing onto something aspiring—to pull us out of the mental sinkhole of Obsessing.

How This Mind Game Works

Obsessing exaggerates our desire to "get it right." We are *so* determined, *so* focused, and *so* hell-bent on making the right decision that we over-think, over-stress, and over-extend ourselves. We perpetuate Obsessing *because* we are so hell-bent on "getting it right." Obsessing promises that we *will* "get it right" if only we *continue* to think it through. Of course, this is a lie. The whole purpose of Obsessing is to make sure that we *never* finish thinking it through.

We want to "get it right" for all the right reasons. We want God to be pleased with us. We want Him to bless what we do. We want to get ahead in life. We want to be proud of the work of our hands. What Satan does, then, is make sure that our good intentions become an endless source of stressful fruitlessness. The very thing we *want* so badly to do becomes the thing that we cannot bring ourselves to do.

THEREFORE, the fourth thing we can do to end Obsessing is to accept that we are not infallible. If we do make a mistake, it would not be the first mistake we have ever made. We have made mistakes in the past, and somehow, by grace, we have lived through all of them, even the ones we thought would "kill us." The truth is, God has rescued us—*many times*—from the consequences of our poor decisions. Nothing we do in this life is *that* final with God. There will always be another love, another job, and another set of cabinet knobs. Keeping this level-headed perspective of our options helps us escape Satan's trap. The decision bringing our lives to a paralyzing standstill today will prove itself tomorrow, in hindsight, to have been humorously insignificant.

Obsessing works by overwhelming us with something that is made to *appear* much larger and of much greater consequence than it really is. We cannot see anything but that *one thing*. We become fixated on this *one thing*. Our whole world is comprised of that one *mole hill*, and that mole hill is blocking our view of everything else. We are convinced that we cannot possibly move forward until we have resolved this one thing. But this *one thing* has us paralyzed.

The truth is we *can* change our kitchen knobs anytime we want. And books *do* routinely undergo revisions after their initial printing. In the moment, however, our reasoning becomes disoriented in a fog of Obsessing. We lose our bearings. We temporarily lose our grip on reality. We are doped into thinking that, if we get this "wrong," our whole life going forward will virtually be ruined.

THEREFORE, the fifth thing we can do to stop Obsessing is to do a reality check. We should ask ourselves objectively if the decision before us is *truly* irreversible. We need to contradict the demonic thoughts threatening that we will never be able to change our decision once it has been made. The truth is, the Bible is full of examples of human predicaments far worse than ours that God has reversed.

Both my neighbor and myself put way too much pressure, way too much responsibility, and way too much accountability on ourselves. We both temporarily took our eyes off the fact that we are not responsible for making our lives here on earth P.E.R.F.E.C.T. This expectation of perfection is an unattainable burden that we humans put on ourselves. It is a burden that Satan certainly fertilizes because he knows that the heavy weight of perfectionism will cause our knees to buckle.

Perfection has never been God's expectation of us. The Bible is full of counsel on what steps we are to follow *because* we were not created to be perfect. Leave our gift at the altar and make amends with our brother. Confess our sins. Put on sackcloth and repent. Rend our hearts. Return to Him, etc.

THEREFORE, the sixth thing we can do to stop Obsessing is to remind ourselves that, ultimately, making things perfect is *God's* job. Everything *He* creates is P.E.R.F.E.C.T. Everything *He* touches is perfected—even our fallen nature. God can take even our seemingly "bad" choices and bring good out of them. There is nothing that we humans can do that is so wrong, so perverse, or so messed up that is beyond God's power to turn into eventual good.

There is an old adage, "God writes straight with crooked lines." After we have done our best to discern, we can commit to a decision knowing that God still has a bird's-eye view of our lives. Even things that truly cannot be reversed, God works even those things—*all things*—to the good of those who love Him. Trusting in that tenant of our faith will make committing to decisions a lot easier for us by removing the pressure to be P.E.R.F.E.C.T.

Obsessing and the End Times

The purpose of Obsessing, as mentioned earlier, is to prevent us from finalizing decisions and moving forward. Satan uses Obsessing to block us from making a commitment, taking a stand, and/or stepping boldly forward. Nothing will so mark the End Times on earth as these three objectives.

Satan's agenda would be greatly advanced if Christians would simply roll over and die. Whether we literally die, or simply live as if we are dead inside—either way works for him. The mental torment of Obsessing actually produces this result for him. Under-achieving, under-productive, and under-accomplished Christians *help* Satan rule earth by allowing him to gain, steal, and usurp large portions of it without a fight.

Christians are becoming weak—too afraid to step out and declare where they stand. Too insecure to accomplish their duties.

Too vague and wishy-washy to be a pillar of the Truth. Christians are becoming frail—too mentally limp to exercise their authority and force evil to retreat. Christians are also becoming embarrassingly flaccid—too two-faced to stand on the promises of God they preach. We Christians, through our waning convictions, are the very people *partnering* with Satan's agenda to dominate our earth.

Christians who have succumbed repeatedly to indecisiveness during their time on earth will be no more able to commit to God when the Antichrist comes for *his* time on earth. They will be the first to run and hide when the trumpet sounds for Christians to rally against the dictatorship of the evil one. The Antichrist will survey the earth and find so few Christians left standing that he will face virtually no opposition at all. Certainly not in the neighborhood where I live. Satan will not be suffering any casualties on my street!

In the same way that God dedicates a lifetime to each of us—strengthening, teaching, and proving that we can trust him—Satan, too, dedicates a lifetime to training us. He trains us to never know success, or accomplishment, or victory. Satan uses torments like Obsessing to make sure that Christians never live boldly, daringly, or fearlessly. Satan keeps us all doubting our ability to do things well, to achieve miraculous results, and to bravely acquire the spoils of spiritual war.

Through continual frustrations, setbacks, and devastations in this earthly life, Satan wears down our determination to stand confidently for what we desire in the next life. His never-ending torments cause us to lose our confidence, to lose our boldness, and even to lose our ministries by convincing us that we can never be sure of ourselves or our ability to make sound choices.

Satan gains nothing, per se, from the trivial things over which he causes us to obsess. Honestly, the knobs on our kitchen cabinets will not determine whether we go to Heaven or Hell. If Satan can repeatedly keep me stumped and immobilized over something as benign as a comma, how will I ever find the strength to make the decision that *really* matters?

What Satan *gains* by paralyzing us is power. Satan gains *power* over us. He gains *control* over us. He becomes like a puppeteer who can make us dance ridiculously clumsy or, if he prefers, sit off to the side, lifeless on a shelf somewhere, out of his way. And that is exactly where torments like Obsessing are training Christians to stay: out of Satan's way.

Therefore,

when you are being tormented by Obsessing, you must:

1. JUST STOP! Make the decision that the debating is *over.*
2. examine your hidden motivation for stalling.
3. look forward to your life *beyond* this decision.
4. trust that God is still big enough to rescue you.
5. ask yourself if this is *really* a decision that can never be reversed.
6. stop believing that you have to be perfect.

MENTAL

Prayer Against

Obsessing

As a child of the Most-High God,
I speak as an *extension* of God the Father,
God the Son, and God the Holy Spirit.
I *command* you, spirit of Obsessing:
get out of my way, and
stop blocking my forward progress!
I also command your roots, groupings, and familial spirits;
your companion, related and interlocking spirits
that, they, too, must cease their evil work.
I *command* that you can no longer be an obstacle,
stumbling block, or wall preventing me from
moving forward to my season.
Stop driving me to unobtainable perfection!
I *cancel* the power that I have allowed you to have so far.
I *forbid* you from communicating with other spirits,
from seeking outside assistance, and
from ever returning.
Lord, I ask at this time that You restore
my confidence in both Your desire and Your ability to
bring my life and my undertakings
into alignment with Your will.
Help me to trust that the outcome of it all
is in Your hands.
Amen.

CHAPTER 6

The

Mental Torment

of

Nay-Saying

Nay-Saying

What is Nay-Saying?

What I call Nay-Saying is a *programmed* mindset that perpetuates self-defeatism. This is a *learned* behavior. It is the result of years of brainwashing to convince us that we are not good. This discounting, self-deprecating mind game is one that, after years of practice, we eventually end up playing against ourselves. Eventually, *we* become the advocate—the mouthpiece—for Satan against ourselves. Like in the game of Solitaire, we eventually become good at beating ourselves. The origin of Nay-Saying is most often rooted in childhood. However, it can be set into motion at any time, in any relationship where we depend on another for our self-esteem.

Nay-Saying is when we walk around all day, reminding ourselves how we do not measure up, how we will never accomplish anything, and how we are not worth anything. We have lived with these "labels" for so long that, like popular songs on the radio, we catch ourselves unconsciously singing the words all day long under our breath. How many times have we all said, "I can't get that song out of my head!"?

Examples of Nay-Saying are when we get a creative inspiration, but immediately tell ourselves that our ideas are not good. So, we do nothing.

We get the urge to act on an opportunity, but quickly tell ourselves that we are not gifted or smart enough to do it. So, we do nothing.

We get a chance to experience something exciting, but quickly tell ourselves that we could never do something like that. So, we do nothing.

But...

Some people argue that it is merely a fact of life that not everyone is physically beautiful. Not everyone is academically inclined. All people are not good at sales. Just because we fall short in some areas, the skeptics argue, does not mean that we can automatically blame our lack of attributes on Satan. This, the skeptics and I finally *do* agree on!

Just because a thought is negative does not automatically mean that it comes from Satan. It is highly probable that we may think to ourselves, *"I can't do this"* because we literally—*physically*—cannot do whatever it is. Sometimes we *are* simply being realistic. *"I'll never squeeze into that space"* could be a reality. Thoughts like these, the skeptics argue, can be instances of our simply being honest with ourselves. True, but...I would argue back that, while we *may* be too big for that space, it is equally possible that the space *may* have simply been created too small. We should not automatically default to blaming ourself—*that* would be Nay-Saying.

WOMEN ARE STUPID

I have a cousin who married a preacher from Tennessee. He believes that God created women inferior, and that women should not be educated. This is the mindset they have now ingrained in their only child—unfortunately, a girl.

Their daughter was a straight-A student, and graduated from high school with academic honors. This achievement brought with it scholarships to various, competing universities. Of course, she was raised to believe that women should not be educated, so the scholarships were all declined.

When asked once what she planned to do after graduation, she shrugged and replied, "Nothin', I guess." I am told that she sits on the couch all day, waiting for some boy to show up, marry her, and get her pregnant. She genuinely *believes* that is all she is good for. Despite all of her academic achievements, no one can convince her otherwise. This is the *power* of our beliefs. What we *believe* is true about ourselves carries more weight than what is *actually* true.

Satan is relentless in using already-broken people to break us. Out of *their* brokenness, they define who we are *not*, what we will *never* amount to, and what we could *never* possibly become. Satan will manipulate virtually every *thing* and every *person* in our life to instill in us the defeatist message that he wants us to adopt. Satan wins when people like my cousin's highly-intelligent daughter *believe* they are "nothing." Satan wins because they never grow to become "something" that threatens him.

WHAT'S WRONG WITH ME?

In my own life, it was my mother. My mother told my family that I was mentally retarded. Ironically, my "retardation" never surfaced until my older brother—her favorite—began sexually molesting me. Mother had to rush to discredit me with our family before I started talking about the incest going on—*with her approval*—in our house.

I, too, was an honor student, and attended various academic award banquets all through high school. I was also a gifted art student. At one point, I was approached by an art dealer to sell prints of my work on the national market. I was also a musician. Not only had I learned to play a musical instrument, but I actually wrote an entire musical score for our high school marching band in my senior year. I won an academic scholarship to a nearby university. Still, despite all of the evidence to the contrary, my family *believed* that I was mentally retarded.

Well into my thirties I was constantly berated, bullied, and belittled by my aunts and uncles as if I were an imbecile. By that age, I was teaching art at both the high school and college levels in Houston. I owned my own home. I was driving a brand-new car off the showroom floor—paid for with my own money. But my family somehow—despite all of the evidence to the contrary—still *believed* that I was mentally retarded. Nothing I have ever done, nothing I have ever accomplished, and nothing for which I have ever received public recognition has ever changed their perception of me, not even to this day.

The *truth* can be staring us right in the face—*contradicting* what we believe—and we will still never change what we *believe*. Runway models weighing ninety-eight pounds die of bulimia every day because they *believe* they are fat. In middle school, I once pulled aside one of my classmates and, in confidence, asked her if I was retarded. If I *were* retarded, I reasoned, I would have no way of knowing. I asked her this *while I was on the honor roll!* This is the *power* of our beliefs. If Satan can control what we *believe* about ourselves, he can control what we *do* with ourselves. So, yes, Satan has a very real incentive to get control of our thoughts.

For the majority of my life, I was tormented with persistent thoughts of how bad I was, and what a disappointment I was to everyone. As a teenager, I wrestled constantly with why could I not *see* what was wrong with me. I wrestled with this constantly because I genuinely *wanted* to "fix" me! I genuinely *wanted* to be a good person! I simply could never figure out what everyone in my family saw in me that was so bad. My freshman year in college, I had a priest yell at me in Confession that I was going to hell, and refuse to give me absolution! That priest simply *confirmed* that I was bad and worthless to everyone—even to God.

At the time, I *believed* that priest for the same reason I *believed* my parents, my aunts, and my uncles—I assigned to other people more credibility than any of them deserved. Because they were all in positions "over" me, I *believed* that they all knew better than I did. That priest, I *believed*, certainly knew God's heart better than I did. Shortly thereafter, the Church further confirmed his insightfulness by appointing him a bishop! My parents certainly knew more than I did. If I truly was a bad person, they would certainly be the ones who would know. I just could not ever get anyone to tell me what was wrong with me. *Everybody* in my life seemed to know what made me such a bad person, except me.

By the age of twenty, the brainwashing was complete. I had resigned myself to accepting that "something" *had* to be wrong with me. By that age, I was telling *myself* that I was no good, retarded, and going to hell. I had coined a personal life motto: "*Everyone* cannot be wrong about me, and me, alone, be right."

I reasoned that all the people in my life could not *all* be wrong about me. I obviously *was* too retarded to figure it out. There *had* to be something wrong with me. So, I *believed* there was. And, since I was going to hell anyway, I started acting out and living as if hell was *supposed* to be my home.

It was not until my late thirties that I began to realize that it was all a lie. All of it. My whole life had been one continuous, snowballing lie. Everyone whom I had ever let define me was a liar. Everything I had ever been *told* was a lie. Everything I had been *accused* of being was a lie. Everything that was *prophesied* over my future—it was *all* a lie. Even the curse that priest spoke over my soul—that, too, was a lie!

And that life motto of mine?... *LIE!* There was nothing "wrong" with *me*. It was *Satan!*

Our programmed, self-deprecating outlook on life—*always* being wrong and *always* being inadequate—is the unnatural, unhealthy product of demonic brainwashing. Nay-Saying becomes our default mentality because we never challenge from where we acquired our self-defeating thoughts. Thankfully, there are guidelines by which we can discern today whether Satan has *distorted* our beliefs about ourselves or if we truly are as worthless as we *believe* we are.

How to Recognize Satan

To begin with, I have news for people who are victims of Nay-Saying: EVERYONE CAN BE WRONG! I am reminded of my college sociology professor. I do not remember the professor's name, only his big Afro and bushy moustache. I remember him telling us on the first day of class that the oldest recorded sociological statement ever unearthed by archeologists was written on the wall of some obscure cave somewhere. It reads, "The masses are asses."

That one statement, I remember thinking, was confirmed when "everyone" was *wrong* about Noah. And, again, centuries after that when "everyone" was *wrong* about Jesus! Not only is it *possible*, but it is *plausible* that everyone can be wrong. The difference between Noah, Jesus, and ourselves is that we have abdicated to the people around us.

It is not always easy for us to challenge our own beliefs about ourselves. For many of us, our lives have *proven* Nay-Saying to be true. This is the "evidence" of our worthlessness that Satan continually throws in our face. He does this to keep us under his control. Logically speaking, though, the alternative should also be true. If Satan is, in fact, merely manipulating us, there should also be "evidence" of that. And there is.

The first way we can recognize Satan is by the overwhelming negativity of the thoughts we have about ourselves. Satan is *always* telling us that others do not like us, that we will never succeed, that we cannot do anything right, etc. He is *constantly* whispering that we are only a burden to everyone. It would be better if we were dead. No one can be *that* bad. Even Charles Manson had friends.

A second way we can recognize Satan is by his monopoly of our thoughts. Nay-Saying is a monologue. When Satan speaks, my experience has been that he does *all* of the talking. We never have the chance to get in a word or opposing opinion when Satan is involved. It is not a two-way conversation such as we experience in prayer with God.

The third way we can recognize Satan is by the fruit. Nay-Saying always produces thoughts that paralyzes us. The primary goal of Nay-Saying is that we do nothing. We surrender. We die. We accept defeat. We give up without even trying. We do not act on our impulses a/k/a the promptings of the Holy Spirit. We simply do nothing.

The fruit of Nay-Saying is that it causes us to STOP—to shut down, to back off, to run away and withdraw. Satan cannot risk us trying, daring, wondering, or exploring our God-given potential. He does not want us open to the Spirit, to God, to others, to opportunity. Nay-Saying causes us to barricade ourselves from experiencing a vibrant, powerful life. Jesus, on the other hand, came that we should have life to the fullest. So, we have a spiritual dichotomy here.

The fourth way we can recognize when Satan is speaking is that negative thoughts sometimes come to us in the first person. The thought "pops" into our head as if someone is actually talking to us. "No man could be attracted to you." The way that thought is worded *sounds* as if someone is speaking *at* me.

If that same opinion had originated out of my own low self-esteem or insecurity, it would be worded differently. If I were thinking it to *myself*, the thought would sound more like, "*No man will ever be attracted to me.*" Or, "*I am not attractive.*" When we "think" a self-deprecating thought in the first person like, "*You* can't do this," that is conclusive proof that Satan is speaking.

We sometimes say things like "I thought to myself…" or "I said to myself…" Neither of these is true. We need to stop protecting Satan by taking the blame for his thoughts. This is *not* how we generally talk to ourselves. Rather than *reinforcing* Nay-Saying by saying, "I thought to myself…" we would be more accurate to say, "The thought came to me…"

The fifth way that we can recognize Satan behind Nay-Saying is by the drama. Satan is a "drama queen." He can hardly wait for the Antichrist to be revealed so he can, once again, be the flamboyant showman that he loves to be. Satan loves the excess, the extreme, and the exaggerated. Therefore, he can be recognized by his use of thought language that is extreme, hysterical, and dripping with drama. Nay-Saying sounds like:

"I *never* do anything right…"

"I *always* make a fool of myself…"

"*Everyone* hates me…"

"*Everything* I do goes wrong…"

"My *whole life* has been…"

We can cancel satanic brainwashing the same way we learned it: through practice. It almost sounds too simplistic to actually work. Except that is does work. Self-defeatism is not something we were born with; it was something we *learned*. Like any bad habit, we can un-learn it. For example,

"I'm just a…"

"No, I'm not."

We can say—out loud if possible—something like, "*In the Name of Jesus, and in the authority I have as a Christian, I command you, lying spirit, to stop speaking to me! Be gone!*" We must command demons out loud, even if only under our breath. The reason for this is because demons cannot read our minds. They are only forced to obey the commands they hear.

THEREFORE, the first thing we can do to stop Nay-Saying is exercise our spiritual authority. Merely knowing how to build a house does nothing to keep us protected from the elements if we never actually build it. We must proactively take authority over Nay-Saying and command it to be gone.

The truth is something we need to tell *ourselves*. Satan knows how desperately humans need affirmation, and he works relentlessly to make sure that we never receive it. Therefore, we must affirm ourselves. We cannot wait for other people to do it. Other people cannot possibly understand the mental torment we suffer with Nay-Saying, and it is not fair of us to expect them to understand it.

In situations today where there *may* be a kernel of truth to someone's criticism of me, I simply thank God for calling it to my attention, and we discuss it later in our prayer time. I choose now, as an adult, to filter criticism. I use what is legitimate to *improve* my character, but I never allow criticism to *define* my character.

The Purpose of Nay-Saying

The purpose of Nay-Saying is to beat us down to the point where we believe that no one—not even God—thinks that we are good enough. So, we give up. We give up without a fight. We do not even try. Nay-Saying is a mind game that Satan plays, not to turn us against others, but to turn us against *ourselves*.

He wants to so squelch God's anointing and power in us that we are born, live, and die spiritually impotent. Spiritually anemic. Spiritually handicapped. Spiritually incompetent. And he brainwashes us to turn around and cripple ourselves. If we have ever thought, "*No one cares what I think… I'm not going to try anymore… I would probably just mess it up anyway…*" then we can be certain that we are a victim of Nay-Saying.

Satan wants us to *believe* that God created us bad, or ugly, or defective, or _____ (whatever). Satan wants us to *perceive* ourselves as unforgiveable, incapable, boring, incompetent, or _____ (whatever). He wants us *resigned* that we are less loved, less gifted, less intelligent, or less _____ (whatever) than everyone else. Satan knows that if we *believe* we cannot do anything, then we will *not* do anything.

MENTAL

How This Mind Game Works

We learned Nay-Saying the same way we learned our ABCs—by repetition. As children, we all learned that addictive little tune long before we ever knew what an alphabet was! The ABC song is the perfect example of how Nay-Saying works. Nay-Saying trains us to curse *ourselves* long before we realize what we are actually doing! Nay-Saying capitalizes on the effectiveness of the same technique as the ABC song: repetition.

We, just like children, get in a *habit* of singing along with the self-destructive lyrics that Satan plays in our heads. As with songs on the radio, after hearing the put-downs for so long, we gradually stop thinking about the words. We sing along on autopilot without being conscious of what we are verbalizing. Eventually, Satan needs only to strike the first cord and we start singing the morose chorus to ourselves, all by ourselves.

The longer Satan can keep us beating ourselves down, the longer he has to turn us against the One whom we perceive made us "this way." Over time, God becomes, not our ever-present Hope in distress, but the One who set us up for failure. To warp our thinking this way, Nay-Saying's first strategy is to get us to *believe* that we are insignificant.

Most of us, if polled, would probably say that we do not believe we make any impact on the world. We almost laugh at the idea that our mundane lives here at home affect the body of Christ worldwide. Our thinking has become so myopic and so worldly that we have lost sight of the greater spiritual reality.

One little pebble believes it could not possibly change the landscape of the world. However, once tossed into a pond, that is exactly what it does: change the appearance of the whole landscape. Its ripples cause the whole pond to shimmer and refract the reflection of the entire landscape in a way never seen before—changed, vibrant, and pulsating.

We, too, by the smallest acts of kindness, unseen acts of charity, and even imperfect acts of forgiveness can change the status quo of the entire spiritual landscape. And each of us can affect change on a world scale this grand from right here where God has tossed us. Let us never forget that prayer here at home is what converted Russia way on the other side of the globe. One can only imagine what the world could look like today if we had not stopped *believing* that we could make a difference.

This earth is a spiritual battlefield. Every player matters—not to themselves—but to the *team!* Let us never forget that championships are won on defense. For those readers who may not be football enthusiasts, let me just say that these are *not* the players we see on television running with the ball! These heroes are the ones getting beat up on the front line doing one thing, and only one thing. Nothing else. Nothing "grand." Their sole job is to *stop the other team from advancing*.

Not one of these players is expected to make a nail-biting touchdown. Their repetitive, day-to-day, play-by-play job is *not* to be extraordinary, but to simply stop the other team from advancing. That one thing, of course, is never as "simple" as it sounds. Burnout among Christians is so high because, as we all know, constantly blocking Satan's advances day in and day out is not "simple" at all. It is actually quite exhausting.

When we block Satan from defining our self-image, we set him back a few yards. Satan's goal, therefore, is to cripple good Christians so they accomplish as little as possible. He chips away at strong believers to get them to act weak. He mocks and embarrasses vibrant people to get them to keep their light hidden under a bushel basket. *Anybody* who believes that they are *Nobody* will never be the Light for *Somebody* who could, in turn, carry the faith to *Everybody*.

THEREFORE, the second thing we can do to silence Nay-Saying is to ask the One who *would* know to, not only *reveal* our true purpose, but also lead us into it. There is a *reason* God created each one of us. The vast majority of us were not created to be quarterbacks, but we *were* all created to play a role and make a contribution to the team. Case in point: a *lot* of "ordinary" Christians were needed to pray before Russia could be converted. We each have a *function* that we are to fulfill before our allotted time on earth runs out. None of us are insignificant—not to God!

Nay-Saying's secondary strategy, after trying to convince us that we are insignificant, is to convince us that we *had* our chance, but we blew it. Nay-Saying keeps us "labeled" and demoralized by the shame of our past failures. We *coulda* but did not. We *shoulda* but failed. We *woulda* but gave up. And now, that chance, that option, or that opportunity to "be somebody" of value is gone. It is too late.

Hindsight is always 20/20. It is too easy—*and always too harsh*—for us to look back and criticize ourselves *after* we have grown beyond our past immaturity. When we do this, we act like an adult scolding a two-year-old for coloring outside of the lines. Nay-Saying causes us to look back on our *past* self and condemn our *present* self as not pleasing to God. Nay-Saying laminates our past in big scarlet letters that we carry with us for the rest of our lives.

Nay-Saying tells us that if we have not been 100% good, then, by default, we are "bad." God will never bless us after what we have done—or failed to do. We are too bad. We are too _____ (whatever). How many times have we *all* said, "I wish I could go back and do things differently"; "If only I knew then what I know now"? The truth is *none* of us knew back then what we know today. That is simply a fact.

Our regrettable past is *not* a sign of how bad we are. It is actually a sign of our *growth!* The fact that we now view our past differently is a sign of our maturity! Nay-Saying tries to *keep* us punishing ourselves by keeping us focused on our filthy past rather than focused on how we have cleaned ourselves up.

THEREFORE, the third thing we can do to silence Nay-Saying is to simply ask God to forgive our past indiscretions. We must receive this official forgiveness from God for the simple reason that we are unable to extend His forgiveness to ourselves. When we attempt to forgive ourselves on our own, apart from God, it results in our downplaying and minimizing our sins. Only forgiveness from God can render us humble enough to want to thank Him with our lives.

But is it really possible to live without ever sinning at all? Nay-Saying tells us that God cannot possibly live within us, use us, or bless us because of what we have done—or may still be doing! If people only knew... Let us address this debate now, and silence that liar, Nay-Saying, once and for all.

MARIE HEBERT

ONE NATION UNDER GOD

We humans are made up of different *parts*. A good analogy is our American democratic form of government. Our government was formed as *one* nation under God, but with *three* interlocking branches. The three branches of our government are: the Legislative branch, the Judicial branch, and the Executive branch. The Legislative branch *writes* the laws. The Judicial branch *interprets* the laws. The Executive branch *enforces* the laws. These three branches are symbiotic—they work together in a system of checks-and-balances to ensure the fullest benefit to the whole country.

The nature of man works the exact same way. God created man as a composite of three interlocking, symbiotic parts: mind, body, and soul. Our soul (our conscience) is the legislative branch. This is where God's laws are written on our heart. Our soul knows right from wrong.

Our mind (our intellect) is the judicial branch. Our mind *interprets* God's laws. It is our intellect that can, at times, twist God's laws to justify our sins. Our mind decides what is *permissible* for us to do, what we should be *allowed* to do, and we should be *excused* for doing. Of course, it goes without saying that, as with our codified law, just because we twist the letter of law to call something *legal*, does not make it suddenly *moral*.

Our body (the flesh) is the executive branch. Our body enforces and acts on what the mind has decided we will, or will not, do. The flesh has no power of its own. Our body can only act out what we have *decided* in our minds to do.

Continuing with this civics analogy, we can now understand how God *can* remain active, alive, and intimately part of us. Despite what Nay-Saying tells us, all three parts of us are *not* all bad. God remains in our soul, the part of us that was with Him in the beginning, and which remains in constant communion with Him, even now.

It is possible, then, for God to live in our soul, even when our mind (intellect) becomes twisted and our body (flesh) carries out the sin. Anyone who has ever lived with a teenager can relate to this. We all live in *one* house made up of different rooms. Some rooms are messy and some are clean. Our teenager's room may be filthy, but God can still live in the clean room down the hall.

KNOCK, KNOCK; WHO'S THERE?

I believe there is a rational explanation for the gap between what *is* true and what we *believe* is true about ourselves. My explanation does not make our dark thinking *right;* it only *explains* it. I blame our selective hearing.

How odd that we "hear" *Satan* whispering defeatist things all the time, but we never seem to hear *God* whispering. It is not logical that one could "get in our head" and not the Other. God is certainly more powerful than Satan. Of the two, God would be the one most able to do such a thing. Yet, for some strange reason, it is never Him that we hear. I know for a fact that we hear Satan speaking because we are constantly repeating after him.

Most people, tragically, believe that God does not speak to them. They do not know what He sounds like. I have to believe that if people *knew* what God sounds like, they would pay attention! If people *knew* what God sounds like, they would *believe* whatever they heard Him say! But they are convinced that they have never heard God speak. Technically, of course, they have never heard Satan "speak" either.

Most of us have not. Most of us have never experienced hearing the audible voice of either God or Satan! Both God and Satan speak to us as spiritual beings, meaning we do not hear them as human. We hear human things through human means, like our ears, and we "hear" ethereal things through ethereal means like dreams, visions, prophecies, and thoughts.

Because we do not know what either God or Satan literally sounds like, we are hard-pressed to explain why we disproportionately believe one over the other. Why do we receive thoughts from Satan quicker, easier, and clearer than we receive thoughts from God? There is no logical explanation for this inconsistency.

If we do not know with certainty what either God or Satan sounds like, then we have no objective way of differentiating the two. They should *both* sound believable to us. We should either *believe* both or *discard* both. But, oddly enough, our track record overwhelmingly favors Satan. To account for this, there would have to be some influence, some force outside of our human consciousness, or some kind of manipulation at work influencing our proclivity in this dark direction. A pattern of behavior this consistent is not coincidental. It is not human.

We consistently believe what Satan says about us, not because he speaks the truth, but because his thoughts are *familiar* to us. Satan speaks to us using thoughts, beliefs, and memories with which we have grown *familiar*. Familiarity causes us to lower our guard.

Many of us have been living with *his* version of who we are since childhood. It has been going on for so long, in fact, that we cannot even remember when Nay-Saying first started. It has simply *always* been a part of our life. And there it is—*always* been… for *as long as we can remember…since the beginning*—the language of the drama queen.

Therefore, the fourth thing we can do to stop Nay-Saying is to stop the drama. "Extreme" thought language is a red flag. Flamboyant language glares like a glow stick in our memory. It is almost exclusively showmanship, and not reality. The reality is, we *are* good people, and we need to affirm ourselves of that. We overcome Nay-Saying by holding its thoughts up against *reality* and discarding Nay-Saying's drama.

We can often resist Satan by simply speaking the truth back to ourselves—out loud if possible. At first, it may feel like we are arguing with ourselves. When we "hear" Nay-Saying thoughts, we need to hear *ourselves* talk back—out loud. The reason we talk out loud is because people tend to act upon the things they say out loud. Also, talking over negative thoughts will drown them out.

Therefore, the fifth thing we can do when we catch ourselves having Nay-Saying thoughts is to counter them with the truth. God does *not* create bad things. This is not how He created us. God does not think we are disgusting or worthless failures. In fact, the evidence actually proves the opposite: God thinks we are to *die* for!

Nay-Saying and the End Times

To reiterate, the purpose of Nay-Saying is to demoralize us to the point of believing that no one—not even God—cares about us. We have only to look at today's exponential increases in suicide, assisted suicide, DNR contracts, and eating disorders to see how Nay-Saying is dominating the global mindset. By the time the Antichrist appears, most people will have already given up on God.

Satan is not at all bracing for a fight at The End; he is expecting people to *run* to him willingly. The Antichrist will not come to win over the hearts of men but will simply come and present himself as the alternative to the God whom people perceive has abandoned them since birth.

The majority of people in the End Times—many of whom are Christians—will gladly hand over their souls to the Antichrist. After a lifetime of feeling short-changed by God, they will *rush* to be sheltered in the shadow, not of the Almighty, but of the Darkness that guarantees their long-awaited vengeance, vindication, and affirmation. Men will throw themselves at the feet of the one who promises to right the lifetime of wrongs they believe came from God. The Antichrist will be perceived as the hero who rescues the downtrodden, misjudged, and unappreciated. The Antichrist will be the proverbial Daddy Warbucks who adopts every Orphaned Annie, and lavishes them with all the riches, power, and fame that thirty pieces of silver can buy.

Those who have never trained themselves to resist Satan's lies of their marginal worth to God, will dive head-first into the opportunity to finally *be* somebody, and to find a "family" where they can finally *belong*. They will finally be vindicated for their righteousness, and command the respect of everyone who has ever disregarded them. All of their heart's longings will finally be satisfied. Every tear will be wiped away. Pain and suffering will be no more. For many people, the coming of the Antichrist will sound a lot like Heaven.

MARIE HEBERT

Therefore,

when you are being tormented by Nay-Saying, you must:

1. command the demons to shut up.
2. ask God to reveal your purpose and to use you.
3. seek God's forgiveness for your past, and make a fresh start.
4. stop the drama and be realistic.
5. remind yourself that God created you the way you are for a purpose.

MENTAL

Prayer Against

Nay-Saying

I assert my Christian authority over you,
you demon of Nay-Saying
as well as over all of your roots, groupings, and familial spirits;
and over all of your companion, related and interlocking spirits.
I *forbid* you to continue lying to me about my identity.
I *forbid* you to continue sabotaging my awareness of
God's love, God's gifts, and God's plan for my life.
You are no longer allowed to define who I am.
I *rescind, nullify,* and *disavow*
any prior credibility I have given to you,
or to those whom you have manipulated,
No longer can you speak to me, directly or indirectly.
I *forbid* you from communicating with other spirits,
from seeking outside assistance, and
from ever returning.
I also cancel every assignment of Nay-Saying,
whether intentional or unintentional,
that I may have attached to someone else.
Lord, I ask forgiveness for being blinded
to all Your goodness in creating me,
and I thank You now for the life I have before me.
Amen.

CHAPTER 7

Commanding Demons

Commanding Demons

RECOGNIZING DEMONS

There is great value in *recognizing*. Recognizing something gives us power over it. We gain power and authority over spirits when we *acknowledge* them because we are no longer ignoring them. We are no longer tolerating their presence. We are no longer running from them. By recognizing demons, we are holding them accountable.

Once we recognize that demons are the cause of so much of our everyday, routine anguish, we become empowered to channel our energy directly at them. It can be a game-changer. I say *can* be—not *will* be—a game-changer. I say this because, just as in all aspects of life, simply *knowing* what is wrong does not fix the problem. We must *apply* our knowledge and *do something* to fix it.

In these pages we have learned to recognize Satan. We have identified five common mental torments that he sends to attack our mind. We now know *what* he is doing and *how* he does it. We have also discussed what he aims to accomplish with each mental torment. In addition, we have laid out options to resist getting caught up in his games. There is one final thing, though, that I would like to touch upon concerning this battle of who will ultimately control our thoughts. I would like to touch upon this idea of commanding demons to get out of our heads.

The first spiritual precept that we must understand at the start is that Satan, unlike God, does not have the ability to be in more than one place at a time. He must use angels to do his legwork. Both God and Satan, of course, work through angels to accomplish their work on earth. The difference is that God *chooses* to use angels and people; Satan is *forced* to use angels and people.

God *could* do it all. God *can* be everywhere (omnipresent), *doing* everything (omnipotent), and *knowing* everything (omniscient)—all at the same time. Satan does not possess any of these three attributes. Therefore, he is forced to use underlings. It is his underlings—not Satan himself—that we wrestle with in the routine course of our common lives. It is, therefore, his underlings that we address when commanding dark spirits to leave.

As part of regaining control of our thoughts, it would also be helpful for us to *recognize* with which specific demons we are wrestling. We want to effectively target the precise source of our anguish. We do not want to spend the rest of our lives struggling with these same mental torments.

Below is a simplistic chart of each of the mental torments discussed in this book and the corresponding head demon in charge of each:

>"What If…"—driven by FEAR
>Second-Guessing—driven by DOUBT
>Splitting Hairs—driven by DIVISION
>Obsessing—driven by OBSTRUCTION
>Nay-Saying—driven by DISCOUNTING

Fear, Doubt, Division, Obstruction, and Discounting are distinct spiritual entities. Each one is, as it were, a "person" in their own right. Each one has its own name, just like each one of our children has their own distinguishing name.

WHAT'S IN A NAME?

In addition to having a unique name, each demon also has unique traits and characteristics that distinguish it from other demons. Spiritual names do a lot more than simply distinguish us. Every spiritual name embodies unique spiritual power. A demon's name conveys the essence of what that specific demon spirit is assigned and empowered to do. This is also true of the spiritual name God has given us.

Way back when God first conceived of us, He spoke His word and His plan for us into existence. The very vapor of His breath as He spoke was the very breath of life that brought us into existence.

Our soul *heard* the voice of God, and responded by springing forth into being. God pronounced a secret *name* over us. Inherent in that name, carved in the palm of His hand, is our *purpose*—our mission, our attributes, and our destiny. In that name, He pronounced our "role" on the team. I will use my own spiritual name as an example.

One day, years ago, while sitting at the kitchen table, I was pondering this idea of my secret name. I was intrigued by this secret, subliminal name—a name so intimate to God that He has it carved into the flesh of His own hand—hidden from the view of the world. I was intrigued that He would have a name—*one word*—that summed up everything about me, every measure of my capacity, and the specific facet of His image and likeness that I was created to reflect. I was just too scared at the time to *ask* Him what my secret name was. You see, Satan had been playing with *my* mind and warping *my* self-image my whole life too.

Believing that I was a failure and a disappointment to everyone in my family was bad enough. But if God Himself were to *confirm* it with a derogatory name, that would pierce me with more pain than I could ever bear or live with. That is why I was so scared to ask God to tell me my secret name. I finally did ask Him, however, but sheepishly, with my eyes cast down and holding my breathe. I really did *not* want to hear it. So, why did I ask?

I asked because I wanted to get it over with. If my name from God really was Disappointment, or Failure, or Disgrace—as I feared it might be—I wanted to know. I wanted to put the matter to rest once and for all. If I really was going to Hell like that priest yelled at me, I would rather know than not know. So, I buried my face in my hands, my chest trembling with fear, and with tears running down my cheeks, I stuttered and choked on the words to ask.

Gladiolus.

That is His name for me: *Gladiolus.*

As I researched that flower, I marveled at its unique characteristics. Gladioli take a beating and keep bouncing right back. They are chopped down to the ground every fall. They die back to the ground every winter. Their shredded, decaying foliage gives the *appearance* that they have been left for dead. But then comes the spring…

That plant is stubborn and defiant—what Christians call fortitude. No matter how many times that plant is chopped down, it rebounds right back. Gladiolus is a Christian who simply will not let Satan win. A gladiolus will sprout right back up from its root. All the "dead" winter long, it gives the *appearance* of having been defeated. However, it is merely rejuvenating and regrouping itself underground.

Come spring, it will shoot up again with thick, strong stalks. It will bloom and bloom and bloom. It simply will not give up. As fast as one bloom is spent, another one opens. And each time it sprouts a new bud, it blooms *higher* up the stalk than the time before!

I do not know which shocked me more: that God had such a *beautiful* name for me, or that God had such a *lofty* vision of someone who had never done anything spiritually significant in her whole life. That was almost thirty years ago. As with all of God's prophetic words, they come to pass as we *grow* into the role. I encourage everyone to ask God for their spiritual name. It is sure to be a mind-blowing, faith-building, game-changer of an answer!

Getting back to demons, now… They, too, have been given unique names. Knowing their names is how we know what they are assigned to do to us. The reverse is also true. Recognizing what they are *doing* to us, reveals to us their names. The whole purpose of Fear is to keep us afraid. Doubt undermines our faith. Division is assigned to break up relationships. Obstruction blocks us from moving forward. Discounting belittles our worth.

BIRDS OF A FEATHER

The third thing we must remember when commanding demons is that demons always work in groups. Every head demon has underlings and subordinates who carry out their orders. They prowl the earth like a pack of coyotes. They are coordinated and methodical in their search for blood. It is virtually impossible for us to know, much less call out, the name of every single demon in the pack. Therefore, the way we "clear our mind" is by commanding the head demon *with all its subordinates* to leave together —as a group.

Spiritual warfare works on the same principle as removing a beehive from one's property: remove the queen and her drones will follow after her. This is why we always include "companion and related" spirits when we command demons to leave. I have provided a sample prayer at the end of each of the foregoing chapters as an example.

Early on in each sample prayer, I establish that I am not speaking to only one demon, but to the whole group. I establish irrefutably that I am taking authority over *every* spirit connected, directly or indirectly, with my torment. I am commanding *all* of them. It is not necessary that we name each individual spirit; it is enough to command them as a group defined by their common purpose.

It would accomplish nothing if we restrained one demon, but let all the others get away. As the Bible warns us, those who escape will simply run to Hell for backup. They will then return with seven times more demons, all worse than the first. This is why I always forbid demons from seeking outside assistance and ever returning.

The fourth precept of spiritual warfare is that we command demons verbally. As we discussed earlier, demons cannot read our minds. They cannot obey commands they do not hear. We include all these collateral spirits out loud to assure that every one of them knows, without a doubt, that we are talking to *them,* and what we demand of them.

As a final note, these prayers are *not*, as they say, written in stone. They are only written on paper. This means that each reader can tweak them to accommodate the nuances and particulars of their own, personal battle.

Amen. Amen and Amen. I say it again, Amen! Let us stand now and reclaim what has been taken from us by way of mental trickery. Let it be done today as God has *ordained* it to be, as Scripture has *promised* it to be, and as Jesus has *proven* it to be. As God's people, *we have God's authority!* And He expects us to use it.

God is raising and training an army of warriors today who will stand against Satan and the Antichrist in the End Times. For those who assume that none of this applies to them, and who think that they will not be here in the End Times, let me remind everyone that the End for *you* is unequivocally coming. It does not matter when the end of the world comes. What matters is when the end of the world comes for *you*.

The last breath we gasp here on earth will be The End for *us*, and Satan will be there. The lives of the saints have reported this fact over and over. Satan will be there with us on our deathbed. He will come at the time we are our weakest, physically and mentally, accusing us and to despair and doubt God.

None of us—regardless of what day we die—will escape the final torments of Satan. If the saints had to wrestle with him on their deathbeds, so will we. Therefore, let us not be caught off guard, but be prepared for what we already know is coming. Let our ultimate victory start right now in each of our lives. Let us begin right where we are—with ourselves, in our own homes. With each incremental spiritual victory we win, we will grow stronger, more confident, and better fit to receive the crown that awaits us on the other side of the veil!

God bless you.

ABOUT THE AUTHOR

A Louisiana native and resident, Marie Hebert is an anointed teacher. She has taught art design and theoretical application in both the Texas and Louisiana public school systems. She has taught students at every grade level from elementary to middle school, high school, and college. Her ability to take abstract principles and explain them in practical, down-to-earth terms makes her a successful writer and charismatic speaker. Today she uses her gifts of the Spirit, particularly her gift of Teaching, to minister to people desiring to live their ordinary lives in the extraordinary power and authority of Jesus Christ.

She currently resides in her home state of Louisiana in the heart of the rich Cajun culture.

Printed in the USA
CPSIA information can be obtained
at www.ICGtesting.com
LVHW091107191024
794236LV00001B/104